WEIRDEST AND WACKIEST WORLD RECORDS

Weirdest and Wackiest World Records

From the Absolutely Bizarre to the Downright Shocking

EDITED BY

Tony Lyons

Skyhorse Publishing

Skyhorse Publishing books may be purchased in bulk at special discounts for sales promotion, corporate gifts, fund-raising, or educational purposes. Special editions can also be created to specifications. For details, contact the Special Sales Department, Skyhorse Publishing,
307 West 36th Street, 11th Floor, New York, NY 10018 or
info@skyhorsepublishing.com.

www.skyhorsepublishing.com

10 9 8 7 6 5 4 3 2 1

Library of Congress Cataloging-in-Publication Data is available on file.

ISBN: 978-1-61608-438-7

Printed in China

Contents

STARS

Introduction

As a child, you always wanted to break a record. You had dreams that you were Evil Knievel and Ted Williams. It's actually easier than you think to have your name enshrined with these greats—you just have to think outside the box . . . or eat the entire box in less than forty seconds.

Compiled here are some of the most incredible records in history. They are strange, improbable, and sometimes they seem completely insane, but their achievements are no less remarkable than many other great records. Their oddities are a mark of avid creativity, and their sheer improbability is a mark of just how exceptional and strong-willed humans can be in pursuit of a goal—and record-breaking glory.

What kind of person chases glory to the strangest corners of the earth? Great explorers like Columbus and Magellan sought mystery in new lands, Neil Armstrong took to the moon, and every four years records are broken at the Olympic Games. For expanding the boundaries of human potential, we idolize these people as heroes. But what if there were heroes all around us, quietly doing what has never been done? Neighbors, friends, strangers in the check-out line or waiting for the train—they, too, could be explorers of the unknown. They might become strange heroes out to defy the impossible and discover just what can be done in the world. All you need is the will to succeed (and maybe a genetic anomaly).

The people honored in these pages have that will: fiery ambition to beat their competitors, to achieve what no soul has ever done. They take adventure to quirky and dangerous places, battling the limits of what's believable and sensible. And it's fun! Everyone remembers the awe and joy of exploring a neighborhood as a kid. The world seemed endless and magical, where anything was possible. Every climb up a tree or trip to the store became an adventure to discover what might happen if you took one step further, or looked around the next corner. These men and women take this adventurous spirit down the strangest paths, combining their personal passions with the iron ambition of athletes. The unexpected always awaits them, and there's always room to improve and succeed. There are always new possibilities to discover, rivals to defeat, and ways to fulfill that curious joy of accomplishing something totally new.

Of course, new frontiers can be both bizarre and dangerous. Exploring the possibilities of human potential is not for the faint of heart. Magellan didn't make it past the Philippines, and Olympic athletes train their whole lifetimes to excel at one sport. But the thrill of achieving something new drives people on—even if it means enduring unbelievable conditions. The record-holders of this book are no slouches. They have planned and trained to reach their goals. To follow their dreams, they cope with the brutal chores of preparation. How else do you walk across coals, or endure full-contact ice? Making history isn't easy.

Everybody has quirks. You might have an unearthly love of Mars Bars, or be able to bend your elbow in all kinds of weird positions, creeping out your friends. Maybe you really enjoy kitchen chemistry. Or you love cats . . . a lot. But when one of these quirks becomes an idea, and the idea takes hold of the right person—something remarkable happens. After inhaling a bag of candy, your friend makes a crack: “How much could you eat, seriously?” Your microwave explodes with little grape fires. The cats begin to breed. An idea sparks ambition, and creativity takes over. Someone will build a remarkable device and they will think up the perfect situation. Passions take time and energy, but these people will do whatever it takes. There could be record-holders all around you, excelling at something strange and hard, but never impossible.

Whether or not they set out for glory at the start—it's waiting at the end. Just like the many heroes and villains we read about in school, these men and women deserve their fame. Napoleon may have built himself monuments to be remembered, but he doesn't have a record to his name. And his ability to run hurdles in flippers would have been minimal, at best. Traditional history will always be recorded, but it's the nooks and crannies of culture where we find real people and incredible accomplishments. These not-so-ordinary people have won their glory with natural talent, hard work, and ingenuity. They've seen the potential just waiting in daily life taken to extreme proportions. They're weird and wacky, but they deserve glory for their exploits—and they have the records to prove they're exceptional.

The world is a vast, strange place, and it's ready for history to be rewritten. So what better way to honor its remarkable oddness than by recording all its bizarre and brilliant records? You might laugh, be awed, or even feel the impulse to set a record yourself. Records were made to be broken, so if you dare, go out there and do something extremely weird and wacky. Hey, it might even get you into our next edition!

Team Achievements

1

Sometimes the pursuit of glory just can't be done alone. Alexander the Great wasn't so great without his armies, and Magellan was never sailing alone. The 1972 Miami Dolphins didn't go undefeated playing singles tennis. These epic figures counted on the people around them day after day—a crew to man the sails, or a team to block the rush.

Bringing things back down from the lofty heights of history—you can't have a 100 yard egg toss with yourself. You need a partner, a friend, even a whole team to accomplish something great and unprecedented. You need someone who is willing to get their clothing covered in egg yolk (being able to catch helps, too).

And those people who set out to find greatness together can not only realize their goals, but also gain something valuable (besides the glory, of course). Most of us have experienced it too, whether we realize it or not. If you've ever been on a team, in a band, or even just paired up with someone for work or school, you've probably felt it. Whether your little league team was terrible or you played D1 soccer, whether you played the trumpet with the band or performed a Brahms sonata—if you've ever played Capture the Flag and been rescued from the jail by a friend—you've felt it. Teamwork in all its forms creates a bond among the participants. All those afternoons catching pop flies start to do something to a team. We manage to become closer through all that practice, success, and failure—and when you do succeed beyond all your hopes, you get the glory *and* the friends . . . these people deserve to be noticed.

LONGEST MIDGET TOSS

Competing in a sport not to be taken lightly (and under legal review), 4 foot 4 inch Lenny the Giant was tossed 11 feet and 5 inches by Jimmy Leonard in England in 2002.

FAMILY OF JUGGLERS

There are thirteen jugglers in the Boehmer family, who perform with torches and clubs, among other things, and are the world's largest family of jugglers.

MOST PEOPLE ON A SURFBOARD & THE LARGEST SURFBOARD

In July 2005, a crowd of sixty people were able to cram onto a 40-foot surfboard created by Nev Hyman.

LIGHTSABER FIGHT

Over 1,000 people gathered in Washington Square Park, New York City, to battle with lightsabers on the night of September 24, 2011.

BREAKFAST CEREAL VAN GOGH

A 72 by 90-foot recreation of Van Gogh's *Starry Night* was made from cereal by 150 students of Sky View High School in Smithfield, Utah, in April 2010.

EGG TOSS

Nathaniel Jones and a friend tossed an egg 102 yards in August 2010.

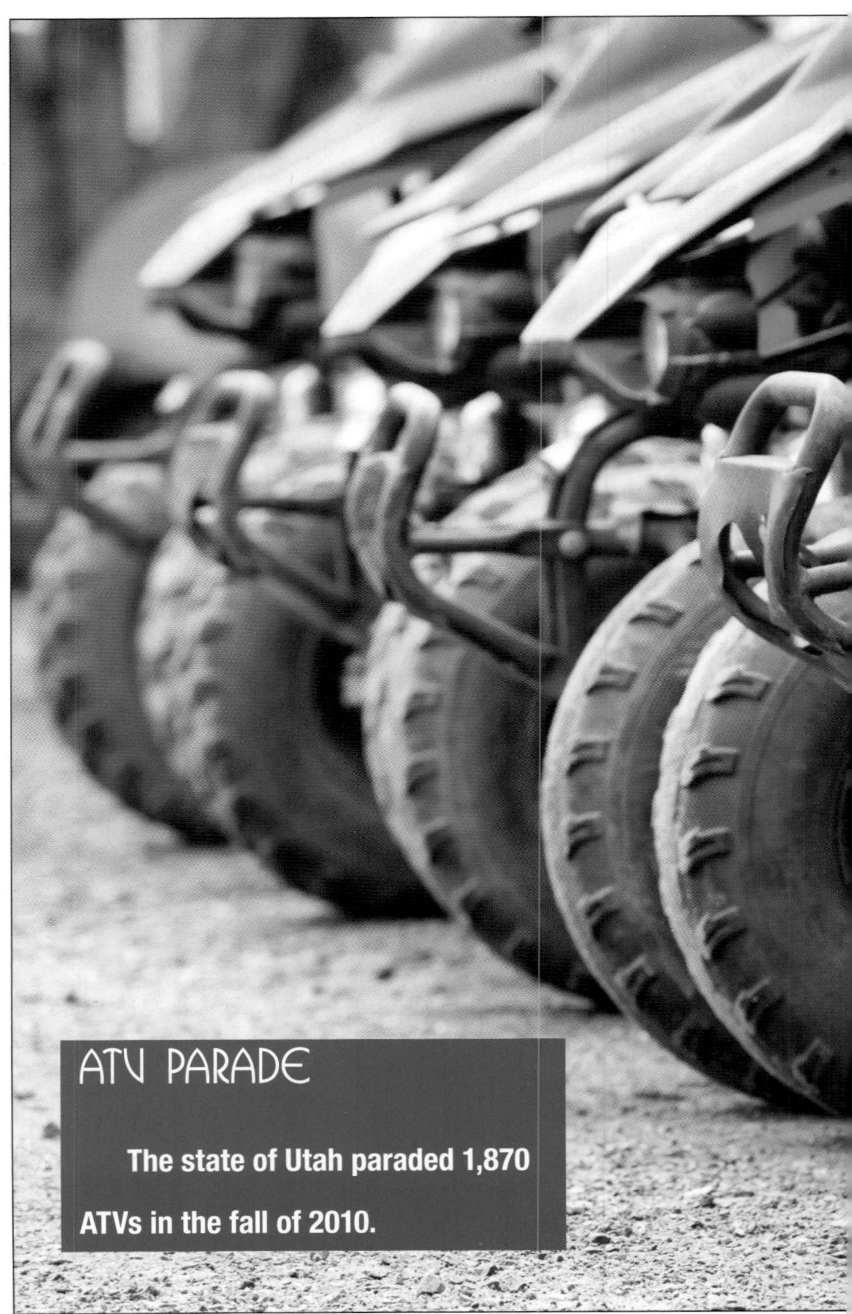

ATV PARADE

The state of Utah paraded 1,870 ATVs in the fall of 2010.

AT 21X7-10

CADILLAC PARADE

Barton, Vermont, paraded 298 Cadillacs in August 2011.

EGG & SPOON RACE

In West Yorkshire, England, more than 1,300 people participated in an egg and spoon race over 100 meters in April 2011.

THREE-LEGGED RACE

Lawson Robertson and Harry L. Hillman finished a 100-yard three-legged race in a time of 11 seconds in New York on April 25, 1909.

MAN-POWERED SUBMARINE

In Montreal, Canada, students at the School of Higher Technology created and raced human-powered submarines at record speeds:

One-Man—7.192 knots—the *Omer 4*

Two-Man—8.035 knots—the *Omer 5*

One-Man, No Propeller—4.642 knots—the *Omer 6*

PUMPKIN BOAT RACE

The town of Ludwigsburg, Germany, launched a dozen boats made out of pumpkins to race across their lake in September 2010.

BED RACE

In Knaresborough, England, June 2011, ninety teams participated in the annual Bed Race, in which six runners pull a bed with one sitting on it.

HUMAN SMILEY FACE

The city of Chelyabinsk, Russia, organized to make a smiley face visible from space in September 2008.

MASS WEDDING

Twenty thousand people were wed at the Sun Moon University Campus, officiated by the Reverend Sun Myung Moon in Seoul, South Korea, in October 2009.

NUDE GATHERING

In Sydney, Australia, on March 1, 2010, 5,200 people arrived without clothes at the Sydney Opera House.

PROFESSIONAL SNOWBALL FIGHT

At the Yukigassen (snowball battle) championship in Japan, 128 teams competed in 2010.

Don Walsh and Jacque Piccard dove seven miles to the bottom of the Mariana Trench in January 1960 using the *Trieste*, a deep-sea bathysphere.

BALLOONS LAUNCHED

Hot air balloons filled the sky at the Albuquerque International Balloon Fiesta, New Mexico, when 345 balloons were launched in an hour in October 2011.

MASS HULA HOOPING

In Taiwan, 2,496 people organized to collectively hula hoop on August 20, 2011.

CONSECUTIVE NUTSHOTS

"Nasty the Horse" received sixty-three consecutive blows to the crotch in December 2010.

FIRST TO KAYAK ACROSS THE TASMAN SEA

James Castrission and Justin Jones traveled 2,050 miles by kayak, for sixty-two days, from Australia to New Zealand, arriving in January 2008.

CROWD SURFING

Giel Beelen was suspended for 2 hours, 3 minutes, and 30 seconds in Hilversum, the Netherlands, in March 2011.

PAPER FOLDING

In Southborough, Massachusetts, fifteen students at St. Mark's School went to MIT and folded a 13,000-foot long roll of toilet paper in half—thirteen times—in April 2011.

FASTEST JOURNEY TO THE SOUTH POLE

Kevin Vallely, Ray Zahab, and Richard Weber traveled 680 miles by foot, skis, and snowshoes to reach the South Pole in 33 days, 23 hours, and 30 minutes.

PEOPLE WEARING SANTA HATS

On November 20, 2011, in Brockton, Massachusetts, 1,792 people gathered wearing Santa hats.

Are You Serious?!

2

Like wolves hungry for a kill, there are two types of record setters—those who move in packs and those who hunt alone. The records in "Physical Feats" and "Feats of Nature" have been set by wolves of the second kind—wolves for whom "What big ears you have!" is just, "The biggest teeth, my dear, all the better to pull this train 100 meters with . . ."

Physical Feats

For these lone wolves, teamwork was just never part of their nature. They have worked with the persistence of hungry animals and are not going to share the glory. Strength, endurance, and fortitude are their fortes—and long hours of concentration and practice have honed their bodies and minds into unbelievable vehicles of purpose. And that purpose is to break a record. Where others have found the task too heavy, painful, or difficult, these individuals have powered forward and become champions of the physical world.

FASTEST DRUMMING

Art Verdi from Orange, New Jersey, holds the record for World's Fastest Drummer with 1,100 drum strokes in 60 seconds.

OLDEST MULTI-RECORD HOLDER

Olga Kotelko is ninety-one years old and holds twenty-three track records (in the ninety-plus in age category)! Her success has led scientists to study her abilities in hopes of finding out how some bodies age at a predictable rate and others don't.

LARGEST WAVE EVER SURFED

Garrett McNamara holds the world record for the largest wave ever surfed, a ninety-foot wave in Nazare, Portugal.

DISTANCE SNIPER SHOT

Craig Harrison, a British corporal, holds the record for long distance sniper shot at a distance of 8,120 feet or 1.52 miles.

RALLY CAR JUMP

Motocross/supercross racer Travis Pastrana set the world record for a rally car jump on December 31, 2009, flying his Subaru 269 feet over water and landing on a barge in the harbor of Long Beach, California.

KAYAK DESCENT

Tyler Bradt plunged 186 feet in less than four seconds over Palouse Falls in eastern Washington and set a world record for a kayak descent, crushing the old record of 127 feet.

DIVE WITHOUT FINS

New Zealander William Trubridge dived 100 meters with no fins and only a single breath of air on December 12, 2010, in the Bahamas to set the world record.

DEEPEST SOLO DIVE

Nuno Gomes is the current deepest dive world record holder, diving 318.25 meters in 2008.

YOUNGEST TO SAIL AROUND THE WORLD

At age seventeen, Zac Sunderland became the youngest person to sail around the world after a year in his thirty-six-foot sailboat named the Intrepid and covering 27,500 miles, dealing with pirates and severe storms along the way.

LONGEST WHEELBARROW JOURNEY

David Baird holds the record for longest wheelbarrow journey with a 112-day journey across Australia, traveling 4,115 kilometers or 2,557 miles on foot to raise money for breast and prostate cancer research.

HIGHEST CLIFF JUMP

Norwegian Fred Syversen unintentionally dropped 107 meters (351 feet) in 2007 while filming a skiing movie, landing with only minor injury, to secure the world record for largest cliff jump.

Fourteen firewalkers in St. Lorezen, Austria, walked a distance of 250 meters over burning coals in 2003 to set a record.

LONGEST AIRSAILING

Dean S. Potter set a world record in 2009 by jumping off a high face of Switzerland's Eiger in a wingsuit and sailing for almost 3 minutes—
9,000 feet vertically and four miles horizontally.

FISHING WITH A BARBIE ROD & REEL

David Hayes, from North Carolina, has set a fishing record for largest catfish, catching one weighing 21 pounds, 1 ounce with his granddaughter's pink Barbie rod and reel.

PULLING A TRAIN WITH TEETH

In 1985, Georges Christen from Luxembourg pulled a 20.5-ton railway carriage with his teeth for 220 yards.

COAL CARRYING

David Jones of Meltham holds the world record for best time in a coal-carrying race held every Easter Monday in

Yorkshire, England. He carried 50 kilograms of coal for 1,012.5 meters (1,108.25 yards) in 4 minutes, 6 seconds.

BURIED ALIVE

In 1998, Geoff Smith spent 150 days buried in a coffin 6 feet under a pub in the UK reclaiming a record set by his mother thirty years earlier and going on to break the world record.

POGO STICK RECORDS

James A. Roumeliotis broke the record for most jumps on a pogo stick in September 2007 in Worcester, Massachusetts, jumping 186,152 times in 19:45 hours.

Ashrita Furman jumped the farthest on a pogo stick in 1997, setting a record of 37.18 kilometers (23.11 miles) in 12:27 hours. She also holds records in fastest mile (2:16 minutes) and most jumps in one minute (238).

Stuart Craven holds the record for fastest 100 meters on a pogo stick with 42.85 seconds.

Canadian Dan Mahoney holds the record for highest jump on a pogo stick, reaching 2.89 meters (6 feet) in August 2010.

Fred Grzybowski holds the record for most backflips on a pogo stick with nine.

RUNNING BACKWARDS

In 1883, C. Metcalf set the record for running 50 yards backwards in 9.25 seconds.

Ferdie Ato Adoboe of Ghana broke the record for running 100 yards backwards with a 12.7 seconds run in 1991.

Roland Wegner of Germany broke the record for running 100 meters backwards with a 13.6 seconds run in 2007. He also holds the record in the 200 meters with a time of 31.56 seconds.

Thom Dold of Germany has numerous backward running records. He holds the record for running 400 meters backwards with a time of 1:09.56 minutes in 2005; the record for the 800 meters run, doing so in 2:31.3 minutes in 2008; the 1000 meters record at 3:20.09 minutes in 2008; the 1500 meters at 5:01 minutes; the 1 mile at 5:46.59 minutes in 2004; and the 2000 meters at 7:13 also in 2004.

A German team consisting of Sebastian Krauser, Stefan Siegert, Roland Wegner, and Gene Allen set the record for 4 x 100 meters backwards relay in 1:02.55 minutes in 2007.

A large German team from Geschwister Scholl (School Krauschwitz) set the record for 1000 x 100 meters mass (backward running) relay in 9:51:08 hours and the 100 x 200 meters mass relay in 1:57.08 hours in 2005.

A German sports club, SV Werder Bremen, ran the 4 x 200 meters backwards relay in 2:29.63 minutes, breaking a world record in 2010.

A German team consisting of Albert Vogg, Gerhard Maier, Roland Wegner, and Thomas Dold also have the record for the 4 x 400 meters backwards relay—5:36.40 minutes in 2010.

Ronald Provenzano set the record for running a half mile backwards in 2002 in Long Island.

An American Brian Godsey holds records for both the 3000 meters and 5000 meters backward runs, with times of 11:19:98 minutes and 19:31.89 minutes respectively, both set in 2008.

German runner Achim Aretz holds records for the backwards marathon, half marathon and 10000 meters with times of 3:43:39 hours, 1:40:29 hours and 41:26:13 minutes respectively.

Frenchman Yves Pol ran backwards for twenty-four hours and travelled 153.52 kilometers (95.40 miles), breaking a world record along the way in 1989.

Plennie L. Wingo walked backwards from Santa Monica, California, to Istanbul, Turkey (about 13,000 kilometers or 8,000 miles), from April 15, 1931, to October 1932 to break the longest distance record.

Isabella Wagner from Germany holds the women's records for 100 meters backwards run, 200 meters and 400 meters at 16.8 seconds, 38.47 seconds and 1:29 minutes respectively.

A German sports club, SpVgg Auerbach/Streutheim holds the women's record for the 4 x 100 meters backwards relay, coming in at 1:17.8 minutes in 2007.

Another German sports club, LC Solbad Ravensberg, set the women's record for the 4 x 200 meters backwards relay in 2009.

Antje Strothmann holds the record for the women's 800 meters backwards run with a time of 3:50.7.

Italian Stefania Zambello holds the women's records for the 1 mile and 3000 meters backwards run with times of 7:34 minutes and 13:19.4 minutes respectively.

Kerstin Metzler-Mennenga holds records in the 5,000 meters, 10,000 meters, Half Marathon, and Marathon coming in at 24:11.6 minutes, 51:53.2 minutes, 1:57.08 hours and 4:42.39 hours respectively.

SAND EATING

A mysterious woman in Russia holds the record for highest lifetime sand consumption, revealing that every day she goes out, fills a bucket with sand, and eats it.

LIGHTBULB EATING

Zhang Yujian, a Chinese stuntman, holds the record for fastest lightbulb consumption, eating three lightbulbs in just 120 seconds.

ICE BATH

Jin Songhao lasted 120 minutes in an ice bath to set a new world record in 2011.

PLASTIC SHIP: SIZE AND DISTANCE

Xia Yu of China holds the record for largest ship made largely from plastic bottles, using 2,010 bottles to build a ship 7 meters long, featuring five sails and enough space for a six-man crew. Xia Yu then sailed his ship a record-setting distance of over 1,000 miles to Shanghai over the span of four months.

PULLING CARS WITH HAIR

Zhang Tingting, a popular kung-fu artist turned Buddhist nun, towed eight cars for a length of 20 meters in August 2009, setting a world record.

ULTIMATE ANGLER

In 2010, Californian Steve Wozniak broke a fishing record by becoming the first person in the world to catch 1,000 different species of fish.

ROLLERBLADES JUMP

Frenchman Taig Khris set a new world record for longest jump on rollerblades after launching himself off a 150 meter-long ramp and achieved a distance of 29 meters. Khris also holds the record highest jump at 12.5 meters (41 feet).

OLDEST MARATHON RUNNER

Fauja Singh, from East London, has become the world's oldest marathon runner—at age 100—after completing the Toronto Waterfront Marathon in eight hours, 25 minutes, and 16 seconds.

SOFAS EATEN

Adele Edwards of Florida has eaten her way through eight settees and five chairs, consuming almost 16 stone of cushion in the process, and setting a world record.

RAMP-TO-RAMP CAR JUMP

Daredevil and stunt driver Tanner Foust successfully broke a distance record with his 332 feet ramp-to-ramp jump in an over-sized Hot Wheels truck at the 2011 Indianapolis 500.

PULLING A TRUCK WITH GENITALS

Tu Jin-Sheng, a martial arts grandmaster of Iron Crotch from Taiwan, pulled a truck with his genitals in 2005, setting a record.

PULLING A JET

Manjit Singh pulled a Jet weighing approximately 7.4 tons 12 feet at the East Midlands Airport, United Kingdom, in 2007.

LOUDEST CLAP

Zhang Quan's claps measure a record-setting 107 decibels, almost as loud as whirling helicopter blades. Officials say Zhang is so loud, he may face arrest if he claps too often.

QUARTERS IN BELLY BUTTON

A man by the name of Randon set the current record for quarters inserted into his belly button with twenty in August 2010.

FASTEST TIME TO SOLVE A RUBIK'S CUBE

Australian Feliks Zemdegs has solved a Rubik's Cube in a record-breaking 5.66 seconds.

SMASHING PLATES ON FOREHEAD

A man known by the moniker "Big D" holds a record for smashing plates on his head with fifty-six plates smashed in 54.24 seconds.

PLATE SPINNING

A man known publicly as "The Great Davido" set the world record for most plates spun at one time with 108 plates in 1996.

BRICK BREAKING

Moses Suhail, a sixth-degree black belt in tae kwon do, fourth-degree in karate, and a kung fu expert, holds the record for breaking thirty-six cement bricks with his hands.

DRIVING THROUGH GLASS

Stuntman Rocky Taylor drove a BMW through a 19 feet 69 inches by 13 feet 12 inches sheet of breakaway glass to break a record previously set during the filming of *James Bond: Die Another Day.*

BENCH PRESS

Ryan Kennelly holds the record for heaviest bench press with a 1,075-pound press in 2008.

100 METER SPRINT

Jamaican Olympian Usain Bolt currently holds the record for the fastest 100 meter sprint, breaking the record in 2009 with a time of 9.58 seconds.

DISTANCE RUNNING

Ultra-distance runner Yiannis Kourous holds the record for running 1,000 miles in 10 days, 10 hours, 30 minutes, and 26 seconds.

PUSH-UPS

Minoru Yoshida performed 10,507 push-ups in a single session, setting the record for nonstop push-ups.

MOTORCYCLE JUMP

Robbie Maddison set the record for longest motorcycle jump in 2008 with a jump of 350.98 feet.

HIGHEST FREE FALL

Joseph William Kittinger II, a former U.S. Air Force pilot, jumped from a helium balloon at a height of 102,800 feet in 1960, setting the record for highest free fall.

BIKING DOWN A NATURAL SLOPE

Markus Stockl hit a top speed of 102 mph while bicycling down the side of a 2,388-foot volcano, breaking a speed record.

BED MAKING

Housekeeper Louise Waller took 95 seconds to make a bed (professionally) at an event in London in 2011.

TIRE DEADLIFT

Benedikt Magnusson set a world record in 2008 for 1,100-pound Tire Deadlift.

MOST-TATTOOED COUPLE

Jacqui Moore and her new boyfriend have a record-setting amount of tattoos with Jacqui having only 15 percent of her body uncovered.

YOUNGEST TO CLIMB EVEREST

Californian Jordan Romero set the record for youngest person to climb Everest in 2010 when he was just thirteen.

MARATHON RUNNING & JUGGLING

Bob Evans ran a 16:51 5K while juggling on October 29, 2011, in Nashville, Tennessee.

LONGEST TIME WITHOUT SLEEP

Vietnamese man Thai Ngoc has not slept since 1973—thirty-eight years in total.

PUSHBIKE SPEED RECORD

Canadian Sam Whittingham pedaled his specialized pushbike to a speed of 82.4 mph.

FEATS OF NATURE

Sometimes record-setters really *are* wolves. Huge, terrifying wolves discovered deep in the Alaskan wilderness. Also: snails, mushrooms, and dandelions. Not to be outdone, Mother Nature herself often claims the weirdest and most mind-boggling records. These flora and fauna have reached epic proportions and are some of the most remarkable things on earth, including the biggest living thing on earth (and it's not a whale). More monsters are out there, waiting to be discovered, lurking where few people dare to tread—or sometimes being grown right in your backyard garden, just waiting to be made into the greatest pumpkin pie of all time! Charlie Brown and Linus would never know what hit 'em. Never underestimate Nature—she'll surprise you at every turn.

BIGGEST PUMPKIN

Jim and Kelsey Bryson grew a 1,818.5-pound pumpkin in Ormstown, Quebec, in the fall of 2011.

BIGGEST CABBAGE

Steve Hubacek grew a 127-pound cabbage in Wasilla, Alaska, in September 2009.

TURTLE TRAVEL

A leatherback turtle migrated 12,774 miles from Indonesia to Oregon over the course of 647 days.

LARGEST WEB-SPINNING SPIDER

The *Nephila komaci* of South Africa and Madagascar can have a leg span of up to 5 inches—though the male grows to barely an inch.

OLDEST TREE

A tree in central Sweden took root in about the year 7542 B.C., making it almost 10,000 years old.

STRONGEST INSECT

The dung beetle can pull 1,141 times its own body weight, the equivalent of an average adult man being able to lift almost six dump trucks.

BIGGEST SQUASH

Ken Dade, from Norfolk, England, grew a 113-pound squash in the fall of 2008.

LONGEST INSECT MIGRATION

Millions of dragonflies fly from India to Africa each year, a journey that can reach up to 500 miles.

MOST DISTANT OBJECT VISIBLE TO MAN

The explosion pithily named GRB 080319B is 2.5 times more luminous than the brightest supernova and is an estimated 7.5 billion light years from Earth.

LARGEST ORGANISM ON EARTH

A fungus in Oregon's Blue Mountains spans about 2,384 acres of forest, and could be anywhere between 2,400–8,650 years old.

TALLEST SAND DUNE

Cerro Blanco, in Peru's Nazca desert, towers 3,860 feet.

BIGGEST CROCODILE

In Agusan del Sur, Philippines, a 21-foot saltwater crocodile was captured on September 4, 2011, weighing more than a ton.

LARGEST SNAKE

An anaconda at 28 feet long and 44 inches wide is the largest snake overall, though an Asiatic reticulated python is the longest, at 33 feet.

LARGEST SPIDER

A goliath, bird-eating spider was recorded with a leg span of 11.8 inches and weighing 2.5 ounces, in the northern region of the Amazon.

BIGGEST DOG VOCABULARY

The border collie Chaser learned the names of 1,022 different toys from her owners John Pilley and Allison Reid.

LARGEST LUMINOUS PEARL

China has unearthed a luminous pearl 1.75 yards in diameter and 6 tons, which shines in the dark naturally.

TOUGHEST SPIDER WEB

In Madagascar, Darwin's Bark Spiders spin webs that stretch up to 27.3 yards wide and are ten times stronger than an equivalent piece of Kevlar®.

CYCLOPS SHARK

In the Gulf of California, a fisherman found an albino one-eyed shark inside a pregnant dusky shark, in October 2011.

LARGEST INVERTEBRATE

A New Zealand fisherman caught a 990-pound colossal squid in February 2007.

SMALLEST TWO-HEADED TURTLE

Todd Ray of Venice Beach, California, owns Teeny and Tiny, a two-headed razorback slightly larger than a nickel.

MOST TOXIC JELLYFISH

The *Chrionex fleckeri* box jellyfish of coastal Australia and the Philippines is responsible for at least sixty-four deaths.

LARGEST BEAR EVER

Bones of a bear in Argentina were found to be at least 11 feet tall, with an estimated weight between 3,500 and 3,855 pounds—twice as large as the biggest polar bear on record.

OLDEST LIVING ANIMAL

Jonathan the tortoise is about 176 years old and lives on St. Helena in the South Atlantic.

SMALLEST TWO-SNOUTED PIG

"Babe," a two-month-old pig from Deshengtang, China, has two fully functioning snouts and is owned by farmers Li Zhenjun and Yu Wanfen.

LONGEST HORNED UNICORN COW

Chinese farmer Jia Kebing has a two-year-old cow that features a central horn, now measuring almost 8 inches.

MOST LEGGED LAMB

The Belgian Maurice Peeters owned a six-legged lamb, born in March 2006.

WALRUS TUSKS

The longest walrus tusks were found by Ralph Young in Bristol Bay, Alaska, with the tusks at 36.875 inches and 37.875 inches, left and right respectively.

WHITETAIL DEER ANTLERS

The largest antlers found on a whitetail deer were 28.5 inches long on each side and had fourteen points total. It was taken in Biggar, Sasketchewan, in 1993 by Milo N. Hansen.

ELK ANTLERS

The largest elk antlers belonged to an animal taken in the White Mountains in Arizona in 1968 by Alonzo Winters. The antlers stretched 56.25 inches on both sides, with thirteen points total.

MOOSE ANTLERS

The largest moose antlers on record are 65.125 inches at their greatest spread, taken by John Crouse along the Fortymile River, Arkansas, in 1994.

BIGHORN SHEEP ANTLERS

The largest bighorn sheep antlers belonged to an animal taken by Guinn D. Crousen in Luscar Mountain, Alabama, in the year 2000. They measured 47.5 inches on the right and 46.625 on the left.

COUGAR

The largest cougar had a skull length of 9.563 inches. The animal was taken by Douglas Schuk in 1979 at Tatlayoko Lake, British Columbia.

GRIZZLY BEAR

The largest grizzly bear had a skull 17.25 inches long, which was found by Gordon Scott in 1976 on Lone Mountain, Arkansas.

ALBINO CATFISH

Chris Grimmer caught an 8-foot, 194-pound albino catfish near Barcelona, Spain.

LOUDEST PURR

Smokey the cat purrs at around 80 decibels—about 55 decibels higher than an average cat and the volume of a landing airliner.

LARGEST CRAB

A spider crab weighing 33 pounds and measuring 10 feet was caught outside of Tokyo in February 2011, and now lives in an aquarium in England.

FATTEST ORANGUTAN

Oshine, an orangutan, weighed 210 pounds when she arrived in Britain from South Africa (though she has since lost weight).

FIRST CYBORG PLANT

Mexican Gilberto Espaza has engineered a robot that nourishes both itself and the plants inside it by drinking polluted water.

LARGEST CAVE

Hang Son Doong, in Vietnam, has a chamber over 3 miles long, 200 yards high, and 150 meters wide.

LONGEST HORSE MUSTACHE

Alfie, a stallion in Bitton, England, has been growing a mustache for several years, which reached 7 inches as of August 5, 2011.

BIGGEST SALMON

Doug Killam caught a Chinook salmon weighing 85 pounds near Battle Creek, Missouri, in November 2008.

BIGGEST LEEK

John Pearson grew a 20 pound, five ounce leek in England, in September 2011.

LARGEST DIAMOND

Orbiting the pulsar PSR J1719-1438, a diamond roughly the size of Jupiter was discovered by Matthew Bails and astronomers at the Swinburne University of Technology in Australia.

BIGGEST PENIS

At forty-two times its body size, a barnacle has the largest penis, compared to other creatures, in proportion to size.

In terms of size alone, the Rorqual whale can possess a 10-foot long penis, 1 foot in diameter.

UNITED STATES POSTAGE
8¢
PRESIDENT OF THE PHILIPPINES
C.M.RUSSELL
AMERICAN ARTIST
Staten-Generaal
45c
AMATEUR RADIO
5¢ U.S. POSTAGE
American Kestrel
USA 1¢
San Ildefonso: Denver Art M
Pueblo Art
PANAMA CORREOS
Leonística
CLUB DE LEONES DE PANAMA
ESTRELLA DE PANAMA
CANADA
RURAL AMERICA
nederla
CEYLON
Tulip
UNITED STATES POSTAGE DUE
GEORGE WASHINGTON CARVER
UNITED STATES 3¢
UNITED STATES POSTAGE
2 CENTS 2
Merry Christmas!
40c
CHRISTMAS 6
8¢ EISENHOWER · USA
NEDERLAND VERSTANDIG MET ENERGIE
NEDERLAND
JULIANA REGINA
REPUBLIC OF CHINA
PATRICK HENRY
45c
FRANKLIN D.RO U.S.POSTAGE
USA 4¢

Hoarders

3

Shiny objects have met their worst enemy: people. People just love to grab shiny objects, hold them close, and proceed to grab as many more shiny objects as they can. Of course, it doesn't always have to be shiny. We all know somebody who loves Beanie Babies a little too much, or really tried to Catch 'Em All—collecting every single Pokémon ever conceived. Occasionally it seems like an innocuous hobby: stamps, clocks, model trains. Lots of people love cats. Until you walk through that door in their house, hearing a faint rustling behind it, and discover a to-scale recreation of 1934 American railroads, a scene from one of those nightmares when you're always late (so many clocks!), or Catropolis, city of cats. The men and women honored here have transcended the word "Collectors" and have become Hoarders on a truly record scale.

They prove that passion and obsession share a very thin line, but if you go far enough, you can really get them all.

RECORDS

Paul Mawhinney owns $50 million worth of records—about one million albums, and a million and a half singles—fifty-seven years worth of music.

OLDEST GUITAR

Frank Koonce owns the oldest surviving full-sized guitar, crafted around 1590 by the Portuguese Belchior Diaz.

BARF BAGS

Nick Vermeulen has over 3,728 different bags from over 800 airliners.

CATS

Lynea Lattanzio has adopted 700 wild and abandoned cats in her home in Parlier, California.

DOGS

Ha Wenjin, from China, has adopted 1,500 stray dogs.

PS2 GAMES

"Ahans 76," as he is known in the Playstation community, has collected each of the 1,850 original titles released for Playstation 2.

THE COLOR PINK

Kitten Kay Sera has only worn pink clothing for the past twenty-five years and every object in her Los Angeles home is or contains the color pink.

LOVE DOLLS

Bob and Lizzie Gibbins have collected 240 different love dolls, which fill their home in Madley, Herefordshire (U.K.). They have spent over £100,000 so far.

AIRLINE SPOONS

Austrian Dieter Kapsch has collected 1,760 spoons from 447 different airlines.

CERAMIC CATS

Pamela Cole owns 2,222 ceramic cats in her home in Birmingham, England.

RATS

Kevin and Kate Rattray share their Yorkshire home with twenty-seven pet rats.

KOPEKS

In Novosibirsk, Russia, Yuri Babin has collected five million kopek coins, a total weighing 7.5 tons and worth a little more than $1,500.

BEER CANS

A man from Clevendon, Great Britain, Nick Weset, has gathered 6,788 beer cans.

WASP NESTS

Terry Prouty, residing in Oklahoma, keeps 102 wasp nests.

BURNT FOOD

Debora Henson-Conant curates her own collection of burnt food at the Burnt Food Museum in Arlington, Massachusetts.

PENISES

Sigurdur Hjartarson, who runs the Icelandic Phallological Museum, owns over 200 varieties of penises.

BANANA MEMORABILIA

Fred Garbutt took over Ken Bannister's collection of banana memorabilia, which contains 17,000 items, including a banana golf club and varieties of banana costumes.

FISH POSTERS

Bob Toelle has collected 753 posters with fish on them, keeping them catalogued according to species, style, and source.

FAMOUS AUTOGRAPHS OF HIS OWN NAME

Paul Schmelzer has accrued his name seventy-two times—as signed by famous people.

HANDCUFFS

Joseph W. Lauher has collected hundreds of handcuffs, as well as nippers, leg irons, and thumbcuffs.

SOVIET CALCULATORS

Sergei Frolov owns 173 Soviet calculators, spanning the history of the U.S.S.R.

BACK SCRATCHERS

Gideon Weiss owns 236 varieties of back-scratchers from all over the world.

MOIST TOWELETTES

John French, of Dimondale, Michigan, owns several hundred moist towelletes, featured in his Moist Towelette Museum in East Lansing.

CHOCOLATE WRAPPERS

Martin Mihál owns 38,579 chocolate wrappers.

BANANA LABELS

Becky Martz owns 11,268 banana labels, ninety-three broccoli bands, and 157 asparagus bands.

OUIJA BOARDS

The Museum of Talking Boards features over ninety-six Ouija boards.

STREET SIGNS & TRAFFIC LIGHTS

Steve Salcedo, of Indiana, has a collection of 350 street signs and traffic lights, which continues to grow.

TOILET SEAT ART

Barney Smith, of Alamo Heights, Texas, has collected over 700 decorated toilet seat covers.

NAPKINS

Helena Vnockova has collected over 16,000 different napkins in her home in Prague, Czech Republic.

SOAP BARS

Carol Vaughn, of Sutton Coldfield, England, owns 5,000 different bars of soap from all over the world.

LOCKS OF CELEBRITY HAIR

John Reznikoff owns over 100 locks of famous people's hair, ranging from Edgar Allen Poe to Abraham Lincoln. A lock of Einstein's hair sold for $10,000.

HAPPY MEALS

Luke Underwood owned a collection of 7,000 McDonald's promotional pieces, recently sold at a price of £8,130.

COCA-COLA CANS

The anonymous owner of colaplaza.com has collected over 8,000 different soda cans.

KEN DOLLS

Jef Beck of Cedar Rapids, Iowa, has been collecting Ken dolls and their paraphernalia for more than thirty years, amassing hundreds of items.

DALMATIAN MEMORABILIA

Karen Ferrier likes Dalmatians so much that over the course of seventeen years, she's collected an estimated 3,500 spotty things, including mugs, magnets, and bags.

MOVIE CAMERAS

The Greek Dimitris Pistiolas has collected 937 vintage movie cameras.

BEER MUGS

Henrich Kath has collected 20,000 beer mugs in his home in Cuxhaven, Germany.

TOYS

Jerry Greene, who lives outside Philadelphia, Pennsylvania, has a collection of 35,000 vintage toys.

HUBCAPS

Gaston Lapointe has collected over 700,000 hubcaps.

BONES

Ray Bandar has collected 7,000 skulls over the course of fifty years.

MEDICAL PHOTOS

With over 60,000 photos, Dr. Stanley Burns owns the largest private collection of historical medical photographs.

BOLLYWOOD ACTOR

Vishahrukh Khan has covered every surface of his home in India with images of the Bollywood actor Shah Rukh Khan, with thousands of copies of his photos lining the walls.

RETRO GAMES

The French man known as "BryceCorp," has collected thousands of retro videogames, displaying them in online videos totaling over two hours.

GARDEN GNOMES

Ron Broomfield has filled his home and garden with 1,600 garden gnomes in Alford, England.

TWO-HEADED ANIMALS

Todd Ray of Venice Beach, California, owns over twenty-two living two-headed animals, and more than 100 in all.

THE WORLD'S LARGEST COLLECTION OF THE WORLD'S SMALLEST VERSIONS OF THE WORLD'S LARGEST THINGS

Based in Lucas, Kansas, Erika Nelson owns a travelling bus that contains over a hundred tiny replicas of gigantic landmarks.

Sizably Strange [4]

Postcards of famous cities always include their greatest landmarks: the Eiffel Tower, Pyramids of Giza, the Statue of Liberty. And there's always one country trying to outdo another to build the world's tallest building. But what happens when you combine the urge to build with wacky creativity, and you don't happen to be a Saudi oil baron with a lot of steel and money to spare? You get great achievements in modern construction and design! Balloons? Soap? Hamburger meat? No problem.

If you've ever seen certain pieces of modern art, you know that it can get pretty weird—and pretty big. These records are a lot like that, except without pretensions of sociopolitical comment on the sexuality of Balkan miners. No, these marvels of human ingenuity have been made because they're cool and crazy ideas. It's just a gigantic

Swiss Army Knife, seriously. And their creators know one thing: if you build it, the records will come.

TIRE

Beside I-94, near the Detroit Metro Airport, stands the world's largest tire at 12 tons, 80 feet tall, built by Uniroyal Tires. In 1998, the tire was stabbed with an 11-foot, 250-pound nail, another "world's largest," to promote Uniroyal's new puncture-resistant line of tires.

MAZES

Tom Pearcy, a farmer in North Yorkshire, has constructed the world's largest maze, which covers 32 acres and commemorates the fortieth anniversary of Star Trek.

Pearcy also cut the largest astronaut-shaped maze in 2009, measuring 1,000 feet long with 10 kilometers of pathways. In 2008, Pearcy cut the largest Statue of Liberty-shaped maze with a length of 1,300 feet.

CATSUP BOTTLE

Built in 1949, the world's largest catsup bottle stands 170 feet. tall beside Route 159, just south of downtown Collinsville, Illinois.

GOLD COIN

Austria is home of the world's largest gold coin—a 31-kilogram (68-pound) disc worth about €330,000 ($500,000).

CURRENCY

On the small island state of Yap—a part of the Federated States of Micronesia, 4,300 miles west of Hawaii—stone coins that weigh a ton and stand by the side of the road or lean against houses are the common currency, and hold the record for world's largest.

SNOWMAN

In 2008, the town of Bethel, Maine, set the world record for tallest snowman with a snow "woman" standing 122 feet and 1 inch tall.

PUMPKIN CARVING

Carving master Ray Villafone has transformed a 1,818.5-pound pumpkin into an intricate 3-D scene of zombies and demons to produce the world's largest pumpkin carving.

GUN

In 1939, Adolf Hitler commissioned the creation of the largest gun ever built. At 1,344 tons, 20 feet wide and 140 feet long, the Gustav Gun—as it was named, after the head of the family that built the behemoth—was manned by a 500-man crew. It used 3,000 pounds of smokeless powder charge to fire its two primary shell types: a 10,584-pound high explosive (HE) shell and a 16,540-pound concrete-piercing shell—roughly the weight of an unladen seventy-one-passenger school bus, travelling at 2,700 feet/second.

NARROWEST HOUSE

Known as "the Wedge," Scotland's narrowest house on the island of Great Combrae measures just 47 inches at the front—but spreads to 22 feet as it moves toward the back. It was sold as a holiday home in 2000 for £27,000. A new narrowest house is planned for construction in Warsaw, Poland, and will measure 60 inches wide throughout the home and effectively take the crown.

URBAN PANORAMA

Jeffrey Martin combined 8,000 photographs of the City of London to create the world's largest 360-degree panorama at 80 gigapixels.

TENT

The nation of Kazakhstan in Central Asia currently houses the world's largest tent at 150 meters (490 feet) high. The giant tent in the capital city Astana took four years to build and is the city's highest structure.

BOOK

The British Library claims to have the world's biggest atlas, measuring 1.78 meters (5 feet 10 inches) high by 1.05 meters (3 feet 5 inches) wide by 11 centimeters (4 inches) thick. The Klencke atlas is 350 years old and takes six people to lift it.

MALL

The largest mall in the world is the New South China Mall outside of Guangzhou, China. Opened in 2005, the mall's 9.6 million square feet, or 892,000 square meters, makes it more than twice the size of the biggest US shopping center, Mall of America in Bloomington, Minnesota.

CROSSWORD PUZZLE

The record for world's largest crossword puzzle lies on the side of a residential building in Lvov, Ukraine, and stretches more than 100 feet high—19 squares across and 34 squares high. Clues are dispersed throughout the city's major landmarks and when night falls, fluorescent letters placed inside every square are turned on, revealing the solution.

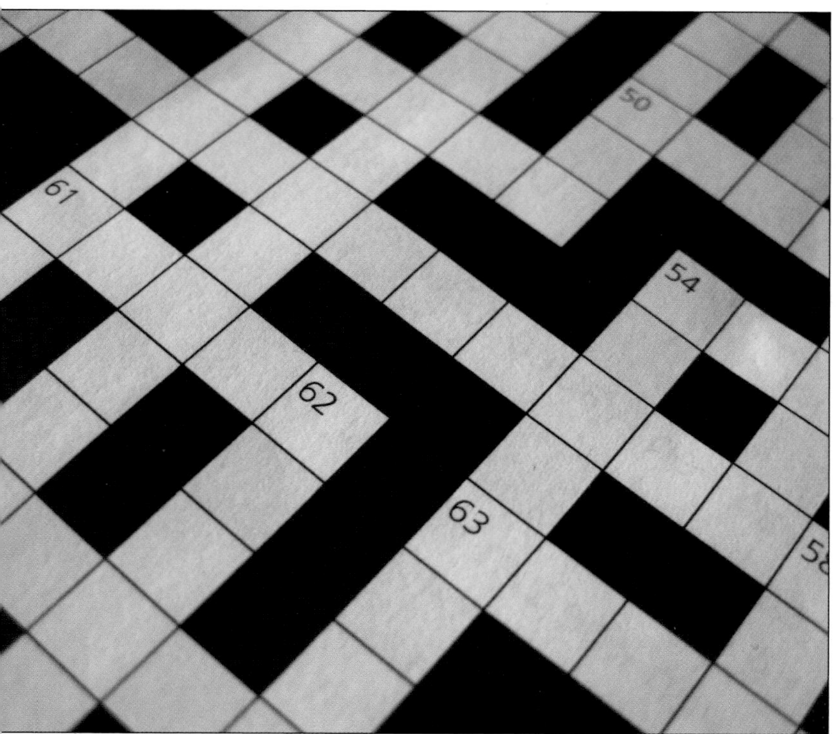

HOMEMADE PIANO

Adrian Mann of New Zealand holds the record for creating the world's largest and longest piano. Dubbed "the Alexander Grand grand piano," the piano measures 18 feet 9 inches in long (5.7 meters) and is estimated to weigh 1.2 tons.

TRUCK STOP

A truck stop between Iowa City and Davenport, Iowa, on I-80, holds the world record for largest truck stop, consisting of a dentist's office, movie theatre, twenty-four private showers, and numerous other roadside amenities.

HOMEMADE ROCKET LAUNCHED

A 36-foot tall scale model of the Saturn V, the rocket that took NASA astronauts to the Moon during the Apollo missions, was launched in 2009, breaking the world record for largest model rocket ever launched.

CHAMPAGNE FOUNTAIN

In 2008, the world record for largest champagne fountain was set in a shopping center in Belgium with a 7-meter (22.9-foot) high pyramid containing more than 43,000 glasses and weighing more than 8,750 kilograms (19,290 pounds).

SMALLEST WRITING

Stanford University nanoscribes Hari Manoharan and Chris Moon broke the record for world's smallest writing in 2009. They've written letters that are said to be so small that if they were used to print out the complete set of *Encyclopaedia Britannica* 2,000 times, the contents would fit on the head of a pin.

TEA BAG

A company, Malte Mate Tee in Germany, holds the record for world's largest tea bag. Going on display in 2006, the tea bag stands 3.4 meters tall and 2.63 meters wide.

SOAP BUBBLES

In 1997, Fan Yang of Canada made a soap bubble spanning 156 feet in length, and using 400 gallons of soapy solution, breaking the world record for largest soap bubble.

The record for largest free-floating soap bubble, however, goes to Extreme Bubbles Inc. In 2005, their record-setting bubble was 105.4 cubic feet and was created with a custom, proprietary wand and solution.

BALLS OF STRING & TWINE

The largest ball of string (not twine!) was created by a Missouri man, Finley Stephens, in the 1950s and weighs 3,712 pounds with a 19-foot circumference. The ball sits in a barn-turned-pub in Weston, Missouri, the same spot it has been for the past sixty years.

About 220 miles (350 kilometers) away in Cawker City, Kansas, the world's largest ball of twine is still growing in size. Started in 1953 by farmer Frank Stoeber, the twine ball continues to gain additions, having accumulated more than 7 million feet of total twine length.

SCRAP METAL SCULPTURE

Wisconsin man Tom Every started building the "Forevertron," what would soon become the world's largest scrap metal sculpture, weighing in at 300 tons, in 1983.

POPPY ART

In 2011, Ted Harrison held the world record for largest artwork created with poppies, using more than 5,000 to create an art installation on the floor of St. Paul's cathedral in London. The artwork highlights the involvement of children in armed conflict around the world.

PLAY-DOH SCULPTURE

In 2011, a life-sized Chevrolet made of Play-Doh held the world record for largest Play-Doh sculpture.

FUNCTIONING SPEAKERS MADE OF BEER CANS

Yuri Suzuki and Mathew Kneebone, commissioned by Red Stripe beer company, created the world's largest functional beer-can sound system, utilizing 5,000 cans.

CIGARETTE RUG

Chinese artist Xu Bing and her rug depicting a tiger—weighing 440 pounds and made entirely of cigarettes—set the record for largest cigarette rug in 2011.

PRIVATE CAT HOUSE

A 9-foot tall cat house in Houston, Texas, broke the world record for largest private house for a cat. Its creation consisted of 300 hours of work, 16,000 hand-cut shingles, 144 roof rafters, 18 windows, 102 window panes, and a gallon and a half of glue. The home is Harry Potter-themed, no less, depicting the Weasley family home: the Burrow.

CRUMPET ART

British artist Laura Hadland has managed to break a record with her over-sized portrait of Pippa Middleton made of crumpets. Using 15,000 English crumpets and over 100 jars of jam and Marmite, Hadland depicts Middleton's face and backside in a 13 meter by 21 meter mosaic.

BOTTLE CAP VAN GOGH

Two University of Virginia Students, Ross Thomas and Elizabeth Farrell, used a record-setting 8,000 bottle caps to create a 7 feet by 8 feet replica of Van Gogh's *Starry Night*.

TREE MOSAIC

Argentine farmer Pedro Martin Ureta used 7,000 cypress and eucalyptus trees to create the world's largest giant mosaic of a guitar in memory of his late wife.

TOWER OF BOOKS

The largest tower made of books is a 25-meter high spiraling Tower of Babel in Buenos Aires and was created by Argentine artist Marta Minujin. The tower consists of around 30,000 books written in most of the world's languages and dialects.

MONA LISAS

The world record for largest mosaic made from cups of coffee goes to an Australian Team who created a 20 feet by 13 feet replica of Leonardo da Vinci's *Mona Lisa*, dubbed cheekily "Mocha Lisa," made with 3,604 cups of coffee and 564 pints of milk.

Likewise, another Mona Lisa replica, made by a Chinese Jeweler, set the record for world's most expensive Mona Lisa replica, using 100,000 carats of jewelry.

Another Mona Lisa replica made by Maurice "Toastman" Bennet holds the record for largest mosaic made from toast, consisting of 6,000 individual pieces

CHOPSTICK FURNITURE

The world's largest piece of chopstick furniture is a sofa made in 2011 by German designer Yuya Ushida, utilizing 8,000 wooden chopsticks.

PORCELAIN RABBIT

The world's largest porcelain rabbit is made from 30,000 plates and was built in Jingdezhen City, China, to commemorate the Chinese Year of the Rabbit (2011).

OPTIMUS PRIME

The world's tallest Optimus Prime (Transformers) statue stands at 11 meters high and weighs 21 tons in Shenyang City, China.

PEN

A Seattle artist has created the world's largest pen, dubbed "Nibbus Maximus." The pen is fully functional and 7 feet long.

CHRISTMAS TREE OF SPOONS

The record for largest Christmas tree made of spoons has been set by a team of Taiwanese students using 80,000 spoons.

LONDON TUBE REPLICA

The largest indoor train set was built by Londoner Jon Polley. At a scale of 4 millimeters/30 centimeters, he created a 20-foot replica of the Abbey Road underground train station in his home after two years of work.

LED SCREEN

In a Beijing shopping mall sits the 250-meter long, 30-meter wide display that holds the world record for largest LED screen. Wealthy gamers pay up to $15,000 for an opportunity to play on it.

FLOWER CARPET

The beautiful flower carpet of Grand Place, a central market in Belgium, holds the record for the largest flower

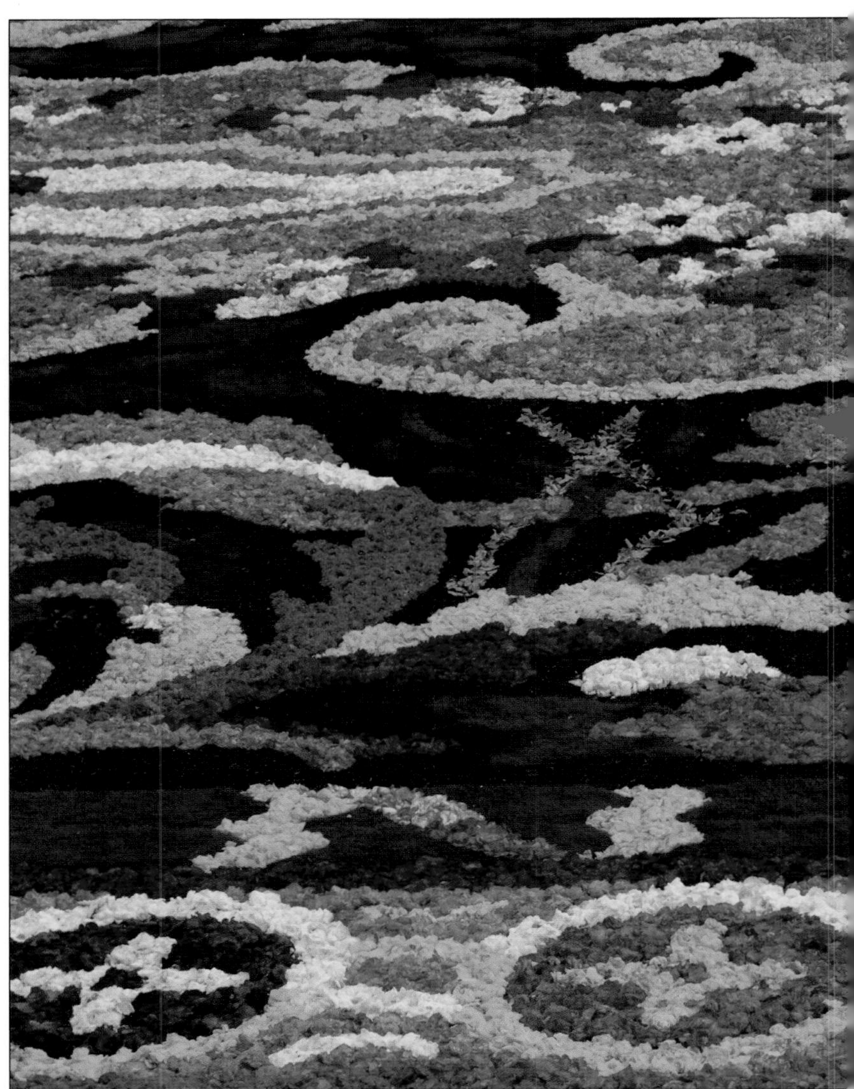

carpet in the world, consisting of roughly 700,000 begonias.

BROKEN EGGS

The world's largest egg-based art installation was created on the streets of Zaailand, the main square of Leeuwarden in the Netherlands, by artist Hank Hofstra.

REFRIGERATOR IGLOO

A record-setting 322 refrigerators in Germany come together to make the world's largest igloo made of refrigerators.

ROCKING HORSE

One of Australia's "Big Things," a 25-ton, 18-meter high rocking horse stands tall in Gumeracha, South Australia.

RUBBER STAMP

A 28-foot, 10-inch by 26-foot by 49-foot stamp rests in the middle of downtown Cleveland, Ohio, commissioned by Standard Oil of Ohio in 1985.

LOBSTER

Designed by Paul Kelly in Kingston, South Australia, a 17-meter-tall lobster of steel and fiberglass has towered over the area since 1979.

TALKING COW

Chatty Belle stands at 16 feet high and 20 feet long and tells her visitors curious facts about herself and her home in Neillsville, Wisconsin.

LINCOLN STATUE

At 72 feet tall, the Lincoln statue, posed mid-declaration at Ashmore, Illinois, is the world's largest.

SMALLEST AQUARIUM

Russian Anatoly Konenko has designed an aquarium 30 by 24 by 14 milimeters, with a 10-milliliter tank, and includes a water filter.

LARGEST LEGO® TREE

In the winter of 2011, Carlsbad, California, was home to a LEGO® Christmas tree standing 30 feet and made of more than 245,000 bricks.

SMALLEST HUMVEE

The MEV Hummer HX stretches only 9 feet and can travel up to 100 miles with no carbon footprint.

TREEHOUSE

Horace Burgess, of Crossville, Tennessee, has built a gigantic treehouse reaching 97 feet into the sky with the help of an 80-foot-high oak tree and six other trees. It includes ten floors, a basketball court, and has continued expanding since 1993.

STOVE

Though damaged by a lightning bolt, a 15-ton, 25-foot stove built for the 1893 World's Fair has been repaired and currently rests in the Michigan State Fairgrounds of Detroit, Michigan.

SMALLEST PERIODIC TABLE

Scientists at the University of Nottingham have fit the periodic table of elements onto a single hair follicle.

SMALLEST HOTEL

The Eh Häusel in Germany has a width of 2.5 meters, and a total area of 53 square meters. A night in the hotel costs €240, or $360.

LARGEST SISTINE CHAPEL MADE OUT OF RUBIK'S CUBES

Josh Chalom and a team used 250,000 Rubik's Cubes to recreate Michelangelo's ceiling masterpiece.

LARGEST IPOD DOCK

The 11-foot-tall AeroDream One, made in September 2011, weighs 870 pounds and boasts an 18-inch subwoofer worthy of 10,000 watts.

BALL OF PAINT

Michael Carmichael began painting a baseball on January 1, 1977, and has continued to apply over 20,000 coats of colored paint, making the ball weigh over 1,000 pounds.

SMALLEST EARTHQUAKE & TSUNAMI SHELTER

Called "Noah," in the spirit of the biblical ark, this tiny Japanese shelter is 4 feet in diameter and can hold up to four adults inside.

LARGEST HOTEL MADE OF SALT

In Colchani, Bolivia, the Hotel de Sal maintains an expansive structure whose architecture and furniture are built entirely out of salt, featuring brine pools rich with valuable lithium.

LARGEST SAW

Plunging into the earth of Kazakhstan, a 145-foot-tall, 45,000-ton industrial saw requires twenty-seven people to operate it at any one time.

SMALLEST COMPUTER

In February 2011, a team from the University of Michigan packed a functioning computer onto one square millimeter.

MICHAEL JACKSON PORTRAIT MADE OUT OF CANS

Seaton Brown, of Wisconsin, has assembled a 144 square foot portrait of the singer out of 1,680 empty soda cans.

LARGEST STOP-MOTION ANIMATION

Sumo Science at Aardman in Bristol, England, created a massive stop-animation film, *Gulp*, using a scene that stretched over 11,000 square feet.

WATER RIDE

Holiday World in Santa Claus, Indiana, built a 1,763-foot-long water ride, featuring an initial descent of 53 feet, at a 45-degree angle.

PIPE ORGAN

The Wanamaker Grand Court Pipe Organ, in Center City Philadelphia, weighs 287 tons and has 482 pipes, 6 keyboards, 42 foot pedals, and 729 buttons.

CRUISE SHIP

The *Oasis of the Seas*, launched in December 2009, measures 213 of 16 decks above the water, is 1,180 feet long and 154 feet wide, and fits 6,360 passengers and 2,160 crew members.

ICE HOTEL

Icehotel, in Kiruna, Sweden, is a gigantic hotel carved of ice that perpetually expands and changes. A storage room alone can contain 10,000 tons of ice and 30,000 tons of snow.

SOLAR-POWERED HOTEL

The Himin Group has opened a 75,000 square-meter hotel in Dezhou City, China, with solar energy powering 70 percent of the hotel.

R2-D2 REPLICA

In 2010, students at Carleton College in Northfield, Minnesota, transformed an observatory into an homage to R2-D2, of *Star Wars*.

MEERKAT

On a field in Chester, Great Britain, a 36-foot-tall statue of a meerkat stands overlooking the expanse, built by Chris and Cheryl Sadler in 2010.

BEER CAN HOUSE

John Milkovisch, of Houston, Texas, has built his entire property out of beer cans after drinking their contents, and includes a two-story house, fence, and shed.

BOY SCOUT BADGE

Hundreds of scouts assembled 1.65 million colored cans to create the image of a gigantic scout badge in the heart of Mexico City.

ISLAND MADE OF PLASTIC BOTTLES

Environmentalist Richard Sowa, in 1988, built an artificial island near Puerto Aventuras, Mexico, using 250,000 plastic bottles. The island was destroyed by a hurricane in 2005, and he has constructed a new one featuring a house and solar-powered waterfall.

HOUSE MADE OF PLASTIC BOTTLES

Alfredo Alberto Santa Cruz, who lives near Iguazu Falls in Argentina, has built a home entirely of plastic bottles, using hundreds of 2-liter bottles and juice cartons.

WOODEN DECLARATION OF INDEPENDENCE

Charlie Kested, of Johnstown, New York, has spent ten years hand-carving an exact replica of the Declaration of Independence out of walnut wood, standing as tall as its creator.

LARGEST TEAPOT-SHAPED BUILDING

China's Meitan County boasts the largest teapot-shaped building, at 73.8 meters tall, 24 meters in diameter, and over 5,000 square meters of floor area.

HOUSE MADE OF GLASS BOTTLES

Argentinian Tito Ingenieri has built his home out of 6 million glass bottles, which make up the walls and foundation, and whistle with the wind to warn him of bad weather.

Too Much Free Time [5]

Boredom gets to the best of us. You might turn on the TV, flip through Facebook, or pick up a book. Everybody has doodled in class or just felt the need to go for a walk. But for some, this just doesn't do the trick. In fact, boredom has become an art for some people, and they take wasting time to unprecedented heights (lows?), earning their place in history.

You can be bored alone, with friends, doing chores, or killing time. But staring at the laundry basket, you might decide to put on an extra t-shirt. And another. And another. Soon you're scouring your neighbor's for more shirts and several hours have gone by, while you're encased in an ever-growing suit of t-shirts that makes you look like the marshmallow man. Sitting at lunch, maybe you spot some ketchup packets and absently squeeze them on your plate, grabbing another. Shortly there's a mountain of wrappers and a blob of ketchup that could satisfy a zombie movie's special effects needs. The question "Why?!" might be screaming in your head but you know the answer—you've been there. Why not?

DOMINO TOPPLING

Ma Li Hua, of China, toppled 303,621 dominos on August 16, 2003, in Singapore.

SNAIL RACING

A snail named Archie set the record of 2 minutes to travel 13 inches in 2001, at the Norfolk World Snail Racing Championships.

TURTLE RACING

At the Longville Turtle Races, 823 people took part in the annual Minnesota event.

HAMSTER DRAG RACING

The fastest time for Blue Square's 30-foot track in London is 38 seconds for one nameless rodent.

COOKING FRENCH FRIES

The Belgian Chris Verschueren cooked french fries for 83 consecutive hours (and over 3,300 pounds of potatoes).

UNDERWATER TV WATCHING

One hundred fourteen English soccer fans gathered together to watch a televised match underwater in April 2009.

LIVING UNDERWATER

Tim Yarrow, of South Africa, lived in a tank underwater for 240 hours.

LONGEST PHONE CALL

Sunil Prabhakar, of New Delhi, talked on the phone for 51 hours straight in 2009.

TIME WITHOUT A NAME

Max, of San Francisco, spent the first ninteen years of his life without a name, until a pro bono attorney finally helped him get one.

LONGEST VIDEO ON YOUTUBE

MoldytoasterMedia has posted a 571-hour video on YouTube.

GRAPE CATCHING

In November 2006, Steve Spalding went to Sydney, Australia, caught 116 grapes in his mouth in 3 minutes, and also caught grapes in his mouth for half an hour, catching 1,204 grapes.

TOO MUCH MONEY

MOST EXPENSIVE ITEM ON THE *ANTIQUES ROADSHOW*

A man from Tulsa, Oklahoma, brought five Chinese cups carved from rhinoceros horn and learned that they were worth $1-1.5 million.

MOST EXPENSIVE DOG

Hong Dong, or "Big Splash," was a Tibetan mastiff sold at the age of eleven months for about $1.5 million in China, in March 2011.

MOST EXPENSIVE JEANS

Damien Hirst teamed up with Levi's® to create a pair of jeans costing $27,000.

MOST EXPENSIVE PHOTO

In November 2011, Andreas Gursky's photo *Rhine II*, sold at auction for $4.3 million.

MOST EXPENSIVE CHEESE

Clawson Stilton Gold cheese is made with stilton cheese and laced with gold leaf and liqueur. It costs $94.83 per 100-gram slice.

RICHEST BEGGAR

Irwin Corey, a ninety-seven-year-old professor and comedian who lives in Midtown Manhattan, has been begging for charity for seventeen years.

MOST EXPENSIVE MODEL CAR

Robert Gülpen has created a model Lamborghini Aventador with carbon, platinum gold, and gems, to be auctioned starting at $4.6 million.

MOST EXPENSIVE DESSERT

Marc Gulbert, a chef in Cumbria, England, cooked up a chocolate pudding laden with gold leaf and diamonds, worth over $34,000.

MOST EXPENSIVE SHEEP

Majid Abdul Reyim, of Kashgar, China, has received an offer of $2.2 million for a six-year-old male Dolan sheep. A dose of semen from pedigreed specimens can cost up to $47,000.

MOST EXPENSIVE PLAYHOUSE

At a price tag of $230,000, a Swiss millionaire has built a miniature replica of his Alpine mansion for his children.

MOST EXPENSIVE CHRISTMAS ORNAMENT

Replete with 1,578 diamonds, 188 rubies, and 18-Karat gold, Embee Jewels London created the most expensive Christmas ornament to be sold at auction.

MOST EXPENSIVE HOUSE

Indian billionaire Mukesh Ambani built a billion-dollar home in Mumbai—and refuses to live in it for fear of a curse.

MOST EXPENSIVE SUSHI

Angeliot Araneta Jr., of Manila, Philippines, used 24-Karat gold and 20-Karat diamonds to construct the most expensive sushi set in the world, with five pieces for about $2,750.

MOST EXPENSIVE KEBAB

Andy Bates of the United Kingdom has created a kebab infused with champagne, mint, and other spices—at a price tag of $1,170.

WORST MISER

Henrietta Howland Robinson Green died on July 13, 1916, worth about $17 billion (adjusted for inflation), and refused to pay 50 cents for her fourteen-year-old son's dislocated knee—which then turned gangrenous and had to be amputated.

MOST EXPENSIVE CHAMPAGNE

American gambler Don Johnson spent $191,000 on a 7.93-gallon bottle of champagne in London, in June 2011.

WORST LOTTERY LOSER

Andrew Jackson Whittaker Jr., won $113.4 million on Christmas Day, 2002, and lost $114 million by the same day four years later.

BIGGEST LOTTERY JACKPOT

Eight Nebraskans shared a ticket to win the single largest draw on February 18, 2006: $365,000,000.

MOST EXPENSIVE COFFEE

The world's most expensive coffee comes from an animal's poop: the Asian Palm Civet (also known as a Toddy Cat). In 2008, a cup of its coffee in Japan and the United States sold for about $60.

MOST EXPENSIVE CORN FLAKE

The most expensive corn flake in the world is shaped like the U.S. state of Illinois and sold for $1,350 in 2008.

MOST EXPENSIVE FRENCH FRY

The most expensive french fry in the world was purchased for $75,000 on eBay and is actually only a prop used by McDonald's in a Super Bowl ad. It is made from polyurethane and subtly shaped like the profile of Abraham Lincoln.

6

Sports statistics are the bread and butter of how we know who's truly a hero among our athletes—who personifies the sport and excels in the top levels of competition. Babe Ruth and Hank Aaron, Barry Sanders and Michael Jordan, Serena Williams and Michael Phelps—

they all hold records that give evidence of their talent and skill. Anyone watching them play can see that they perform, but the records are marks of their achievements in pastimes that we all love. They're the best, playing with the best.

And then there's the other side of sports records. Just as there are great moments in sports history, there are the absurd, the worst, and the most unbelievable records. That's why sports are so exciting: so much can go well and things can go so very, very wrong (as every Boston, Chicago, and Philadelphia fan knows painfully well). And sometimes things just get strange. The same stars that hold a fond place in our memories have their share of weird records—broken backboards, temper tantrums, colliding for that pop-fly. We tend to remember the highs and lows—but what about the strange? Sports (and YouTube) make wacky records more fun than ever, so you can relive the most extreme and entertaining moments of our storied competitions.

BROKEN BACKBOARDS

Gus Johnson, of the Baltimore Bullets, shattered three backboards during his career from 1963–1973. Darryl Dawkins, of the Philadelphia 76ers, broke two backboards in 1979, as did Shaquille O'Neal during his career. Charlier Hentz broke two backboards in an ABA game on November 6, 1970, and the game had to be called.

FIELD GOALS ATTEMPTED, NONE MADE

Tim Hardaway attempted seventeen with the Golden State Warriors against the Minnesota Timberwolves on December 27, 1991.

3 POINTERS, NO MISSES

Latrell Sprewell made nine for the New York Knicks on February 4, 2003, as did Ben Gordon for the Chicago Bulls on April 14, 2006.

3 POINTERS, NONE MADE

Antoine Walker missed eleven with the Boston Celtics on December 17, 2001.

FREE THROWS, NO MISSES

Dirk Nowitzki made twenty-four for the Dallas Mavericks on May 17, 2011.

FREE THROWS NONE MADE

Shaquille O'Neal missed eleven with the Los Angeles Lakers on December 8, 2000.

QUICKEST DISQUALIFICATION

Bubba Wells was disqualified after 3 minutes in a Dallas Mavericks game on December 29, 1997.

ONLY TRIPLE-DOUBLE AVERAGE

Averaging 30.8 points, 12.5 rebounds, and 11.4 assists, Oscar Robertson became the only player in history to maintain a triple-double average during the 1961–1962 season.

MOST TECHNICAL FOULS

Rasheed Wallace was called for forty-one technical fouls in the 2000–2001 season, along with seven ejections.

CONSECUTIVE DISQUALIFICATIONS

Don Boven was ejected from six games in a row in the 1951–1952 season.

CONSECUTIVE 40+ GAMES BY A ROOKIE

Allen Iverson scored 40+ points for five games in a row in 1997.

YOUNGEST TRIPLE-DOUBLE

LeBron James first recorded a triple-double with the Cleveland Cavaliers on January 19, 2005, when he was twenty years and twenty days old, with ten points, eleven rebounds, and ten assists.

LONGEST NBA GAME

The Indianapolis Olympians beat the Rochester Royals in six overtimes, 75-73, in the longest NBA game in history.

MOST COMBINED POINTS IN A GAME

The Detroit Pistons beat the Denver Nuggets after three overtimes on December 13, 1983, recording the highest scoring game ever: 186-184.

FEWEST COMBINED POINTS

The Milwaukee Hawks lost to the Boston Celtics 62-57 in the lowest scoring NBA game ever, on February 27, 1955.

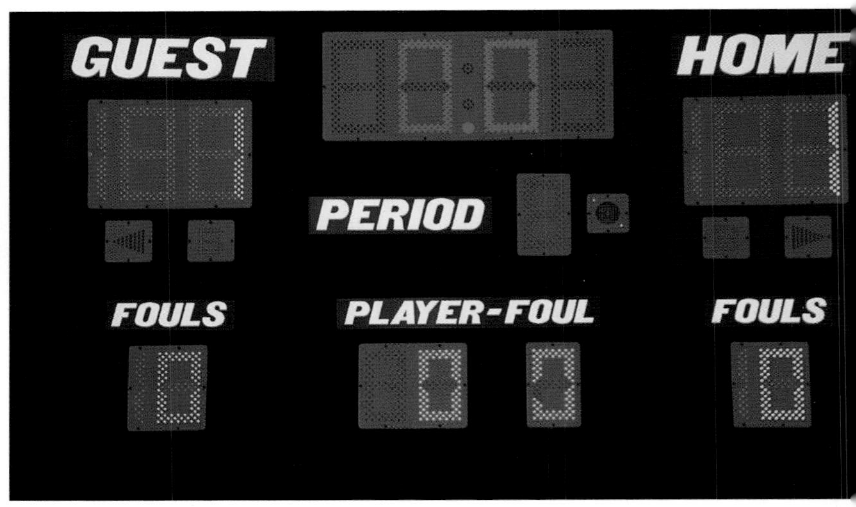

LARGEST MARGIN OF VICTORY

The Cleveland Cavaliers beat the Miami Heat 148-80 on December 17, 1991.

MOST LOSING TEAM IN SPORTS HISTORY

The Philadelphia Phillies recorded their 10,000th loss on July 15, 2007.

ONLY DOUBLE-TRIPLE-DOUBLE

Wilt Chamberlain had twenty-two points, twenty-five rebounds, and twenty-one assists on February 4, 1968.

ONLY PLAYER TO AVERAGE 40+/50+ IN A SEASON

Wilt Chamberlain

LONGEST SHOT

Dwight Howard scored a shot from 52 feet, 6 inches away.

MOST INTERCEPTIONS

Over his ninteen-year year career, Brett Favre threw 336 interceptions.

MOST NON-OFFENSIVE TDS

During his two stints in the NFL, Deion Sanders scored ninteen non-offensive touchdowns.

LONGEST PLAY / LONGEST RETURN OF A MISSED FIELD GOAL

Antonio Cromartie of the San Diego Chargers ran a missed field goal back for a touchdown against the Minnesota Vikings for 109 yards on November 4, 2007.

MOST MISSED FIELD GOAL RETURNS FOR TDS

Al Nelson, between 1965 and 1973, and Carl Taseff, between 1951 and 1962, both returned two missed field goals for touchdowns.

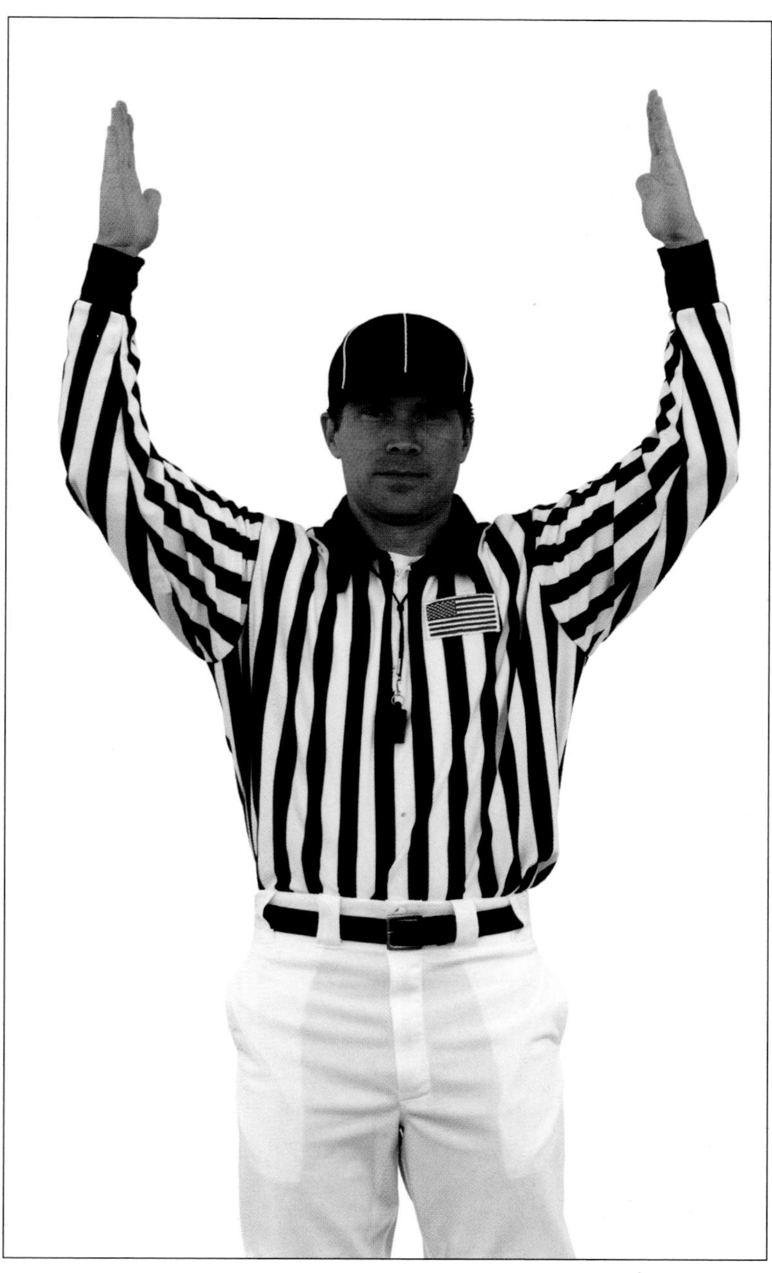

LONGEST BLOCKED FIELD GOAL RETURN

Bobby Smith returned a blocked field goal 94 yards for the Los Angeles Rams against the Green Bay Packers on October 25, 1964.

MOST BLOCKED FIELD GOAL FOR TDS

Kevin Ross, 1984–1997, and Nate Clements, 2001–present, each returned two blocked field goals for touchdowns.

MOST BLOCKED PUNTS FOR TDS

Tom Flynn, 1984–1988, and Ed Reed, 2002–present, have each returned three blocked punts for touchdowns.

OLDEST ROOKIE

Saverio Rocca, punter, started his first game in the NFL at the age of thirty-three for the Philadelphia Eagles in 2007.

OLDEST PLAYER

George Blanda played for the Oakland Raiders at the age of forty-eight in 1975.

OWN FUMBLE RECOVERIES

Warren Moon recovered fifty-six of his own fumbles during his career from 1984–2001.

CONSECUTIVE GAMES PLAYED

Jeff Feagles played 353 consecutive games during his twenty-two-year football career, from 1988–2010.

BROKEN

Mariano Rivera has thrown approximately 700 pitches that have resulted in broken bats.

HIT BY MOST PITCHES

Hughie Jennings, who played from 1891–1903, was hit by 287 pitches, while Craig Biggio, who played from 1987–2007, was hit by 285.

LONGEST GAMES/INNINGS

On May 8, 1984, Chicago beat Milwaukee, 7-6, after 8 hours and 6 minutes—twenty-five innings of baseball.

New York beat Boston, 14-11, after nine innings lasting 4 hours and 45 minutes on August 18, 2006.

The longest game of professional baseball ever played had the Pawtucket Red Sox and Rochester Red Wings battle for 8 hours and 25 minutes, until the Red Sox won in the bottom of the thirty-third inning.

BROKEN BATS

Jay Gibbons of the Baltimore Orioles broke six bats in one game.

MLB MANAGER MOST EJECTED

Bobby Cox was ejected 132 times during his career as a manager.

LONGEST TENNIS MATCH

John Isner of the United States beat Nicolas Mahut of France after 11 hours and 5 minutes of play, over the course of three days, 70-68.

TENNIS TANTRUMS

American John McEnroe has erupted on the court more than any other player, though Russian Marat Safin has only slightly fewer on-court outbursts.

PENALTY MINUTES HOCKEY

Dave Schultz of the Philadelphia Flyers recorded 472 minutes of penalty time in his 1974–1975 season.

Tiger Williams recorded 3,966 minutes over his fourteen-year career.

During a game on March 5, 2004, between the Philadelphia Flyers and the Ottawa Senators, 419 penalty minutes were dealt.

LONGEST SUSPENSION FROM NBA

Ron Artest was suspended eighty-six games after a brawl between the Indiana Pacers and Detroit Pistons on November 19, 2004.

MOST GOALS SCORED IN ONE SEASON BY A DEFENSEMAN

Paul Coffey of the Edmonton Oilers scored forty-eight goals in the 1985–1986 season.

FASTEST THREE GOALS IN A GAME

Bill Mosienko of the Chicago Blackhawks scored three goals in 21 seconds on March 23, 1952.

LONGEST UNDEFEATED STREAK

The Philadelphia Flyers won thirty-five games in a row in the 1979-1980 season.

MOST CAREER SHUTOUTS

Martin Brodeur of the New Jersey Devils has managed 105 career shutouts from 1991 to the present.

MOST CONSECUTIVE OVERTIME WINNING GOALS

Andrew Cogliano scored three winning goals in overtime in three consecutive games in the 2007–2008 season.

MOST THREE-OR-MORE GOAL GAMES IN A CAREER

Wayne Gretzky had fifty hat tricks in his career.

FASTEST GOAL

Dough Smail, Bryan Trottier, and Alexander Mogilny have all scored 5 minutes into the start of the first period.

MOST SHOOTOUT GOALS

Alex Tanguay scored ten shootout goals for the Calgary Flames in the 2010-2011 season.

LONGEST SOCCER HEADER

Ryujiro Uedo scored a header from a distance of 48 meters on October 30, 2011.

FIRST ATHLETE TO RAP AT PRO BOWL

Deion Sanders became the first athlete to rap at the Pro Bowl musical gala in 1995.

LONGEST NFL GAME

The Kansas City Chiefs lost to the Miami Dolphins 27-24 after an 82 minute, 40 second game, in double overtime.

LONGEST NCAA GAME

The University of Kentucky and University of Arkansas played through seven overtimes, 71-63, on November 1, 2003, lasting 4 hours and 56 minutes.

LONGEST CHESS GAME

Ivan Nicolic and Goran Arsovic battled over a chessboard for 20 hours and 15 minutes, after 5,949 moves; it was declared a draw.

LONGEST POKER GAME

Phil Laak played poker for 115 hours and won $6,766 in the end.

LONGEST CRICKET MATCH

South Africa played England during a marathon 43-hour, 16-minute cricket match, in 1939. England was in place to win but the game was called for travel necessities.

LONGEST HOCKEY GAME

In 1936 the Detroit Red Wings and Montreal Maroons played for 176 minutes, through six overtimes, when Detroit finally won the game.

RACEWALKING

Brenardo Segura of Mexico racewalked the 20,000-meter race in 1:17:25.6, on May 7, 1994.

Maurizio Damilano of Italy racewalked the 30,000-meter race in 2:01:44.1 on October 3, 1992.

Thierry Toutain of France racewalked the 50,000-meter race in 3:40:57.9 on September 26, 1996.

Maurizio Damilano also racewalked for 2 hours, a total of 29,572 meters, on October 3, 1992.

Gilian O'Sullivan of Ireland racewalked the 5,000-meter race in 20:02:60 on July 13, 2002.

Nadezhda Ryashkina of Russia racewalked the 10,000-meter race in 41:56:23, on July 24, 1990.

Olimpiada Ivanova racewalked the 20,000-meter race in 1:26:52.3 on September 6, 2001.

JUMP ROPE RECORDS

Jolien Kempeener of Belgium scored 100 skips in the single-rope, 30 second, right-foot-only category on August 2, 2010.

Americans Scott Simpson and Shane Winsor each scored 99 skips in the single-rope, 30 second, right-foot-only category, on August 2, 2010.

Tori Boggs of the United States skipped 492 times in the single-rope, 3-minute, right-foot-only on June 24, 2007.

Luke Boon of Australia skipped 488 times in the single-rope, 3 minute, right-foot-only category on July 21, 2006.

Adrienn Banhegyi of Hungary skipped 330 times in the single-rope triple unders category, on November 4, 2006.

Scott Simpson of the United States skipped 450 times in the single-rope triple unders category on August 1, 2011.

SPEED STACKING

William Polly has stacked at 1.68 seconds in the 3-3-3 category.

Zhewei Wu has stacked at 1.96 seconds in the 3-6-3 category.

Steven Purugganan and Mason Langenderfer have each stacked at 5.93 in the cycle category.

Ryan Powell and Timo Reuhl have stacked at 6.84 seconds in the doubles cycle category.

Germany holds the timed 3-6-3 relay record at 14.36 seconds.

FASTEST SQUASH BALL

Cameron Pilley hit a squash ball at 175 mph.

YOUNGEST PERFECT GAME OF BOWLING

Kamron Doyle became the youngest bowler to roll a perfect game at the age of ten.

What's on the Menu

Everyone gets hungry. Three times a day, every day . . . usually a little more. And when we get hungry, we open the fridge to check out our options, or maybe step out for a bite to eat—perfectly ordinary hunger. This chapter is not about ordinary hunger.

This chapter is about the hunger of men and women who crave food and so much more. They hunger for glory . . . as well as several pounds of food. They have become champions of the table, warriors armed with knives and forks, shielded by napkins, battling history, each other, and indigestion. When you're unbuckling the belt after Thanksgiving turkey, these culinary combatants return for seconds and ask if you're done with that plate over there. Stuffing is a dare.

A world of competitive eating has grown from the long tradition of pie-contests and dinner challenges, and a new

generation of record-breakers have taken to the table. One brave man ate nearly 12 pounds of burritos—the weight of a Boston Terrier. He did this in 10 minutes. And that's

forty-eight Quarter-Pounders worth, to give you a sense of his heroic gastrointestinal system.

In the most counter-intuitive sense possible, these men and women train their bodies and minds like athletes for incredible feats of eatery. They continue beyond the limits of their belts, gifted with a talent for consumption and the will to succeed. A menu to them is not just what you might like to eat, but a list of opportunities in the grand quest for satisfaction. Pride, honor, the title of world-record—food is their sport and the possibilities are endless.

LIFETIME BIG MACS

Dan Gorske has eaten over 25,000 Big Macs, having first eaten one in 1972.

WORLD'S BIGGEST COOKIE

About 100 feet in diameter and weighing 40,000 pounds, Immaculate Baking Co. baked the largest cookie in 2003.

CHOCOLATE BAR

The company World's Finest Chocolate of Chicago, Illinois, created a 5.5 ton, 21-yard-long chocolate bar in September 2011.

BIGGEST BACON SANDWICH

Tom Coghill and ninety volunteers built a 179 foot, 2 inch BLT, with 500 pounds of bacon, in August 2009.

LARGEST CHOCOLATE BOAT

French chocolatier George Larnicol built a 3.5 meter chocolate, seaworthy boat in September 2010.

WHOOPEE PIE

A team of Maine bakers created a whoopie pie weighing over 1,000 pounds in March 2011.

KIT KAT BAR

"Bob" has created a 28-inch, 29.7-pound replica of a Kit Kat Bar that contains 72,000 calories.

MATZO BREAD

Kosher company Manischewitz made a piece of matzo bread weighing approximately 25 pounds, and measuring 25 feet, 1 inch long, and 41.5 inches wide, in June 2011.

LARGEST SUSHI ROLL

The restaurant Umewaka in Japan serves a sushi roll of almost 13 pounds and almost 10 inches in diameter.

LARGEST NAAN BREAD

A man named Mameti, in Xinjiang, China, (with four helpers) baked a naan 3 yards in diameter and filled with 66 pounds of meat and 35 pounds of onions.

FASTEST PIZZA MAKER

Dennis Tran, of Maryland, made three pizzas in 46.4 seconds in 2008.

LARGEST BRATWURST

The Berghoff Restaurant of Chicago, Illinois, made a 47-foot, 3-inch bratwurst sausage in September 2011, weighing over 40 pounds and with a bun 50 feet long.

POPCORN BALL

The Popcorn Factory of Illinois has created a popcorn ball that weighs 3,415 pounds and is 24.5 feet in circumference.

HOT DOG

Vienna Beef of Chicago, Illinois, created a 16-foot, 1-inch hot dog.

LARGEST BREAD AND BUTTER PUDDING

Led by Graham Duckworth of Hovis, a bread-making company in England, seven individuals created a bread and butter pudding stretching 7 feet by 5 feet, with 1,000 slices of bread, fifty-six eggs, and seventy apples.

PETER DOWDESWELL

Peter consumed 1 pint of beer in 0.45 seconds, 2 pints of beer in 6.4 seconds, 3 pints of beer in 4.2 seconds, 2 liters of beer in 6 seconds, and 7.5 yards of ale in 14.6 seconds. Upside down, he drank 1 pint of champagne in 3.3 seconds, a gallon of beer in 8 minutes and 35 seconds, 5 pints of beer in 29 seconds, and 2 liters of beer in 14.6 seconds. In an hour, he drank 34 pints of beer. He also managed 2 pints of milk in 3.2 seconds.

Peter Dowdeswell has eaten 148 prunes in 1 minute, 18 ounces of jelly in 22.34 seconds, a pound of gherkin pickles in 27.2 seconds, 6 pounds of porridge in 2 minutes and 24 seconds, 66 6-inch pancakes with syrup in 6 minutes and 58.5 seconds, 1 pound and 10 ounces of haggis in 49 seconds, and 4 pounds of fish with 4 pounds of chips in 5 minutes and 42 seconds.

ENGLISH BREAKFAST

Steve Magee, of Corby, England, has become the first person to finish a 7,500-calorie English Breakfast containing bacon, sausages, fried eggs, beef burgers, beans, mushrooms, black pudding, and more sausages.

MEATBALLS

Bill "El Wingador" Simmons ate thirty-two meatballs in a minute.

EATING WORMS

Mano, of Madras, India, ate 200 worms in 20.22 seconds in 2003.

BEER CHUGGING

A Swedish man known by Toulouse set a world record for chugging a 33-centiliter bottle of beer in 3.298 seconds.

OMELET

The world's largest omelet (2.95 tons or 6,510 pounds) was made by the Lung association in Brockville Memorial Centre, Canada, on May 11, 2002.

SMOOTHIE

Booster Juice in Kitchener, Canada, took 3.5 hours of blending to make the world's largest smoothie, measuring 195 gallons.

SANDWICH

A school in India set a world record with a sandwich weighing 8,895 pounds and containing vegetables, carrots, and boiled potatoes.

PIZZA

The world's largest pizza was made on December 8, 1990, in Norwood, South Africa. It was 22.6 feet in diameter, used 10,000 pounds of flour, 4,000 pounds of cheese, 2,000 pounds of sauce, and 200 pounds of salt.

SCOOP OF ICE CREAM

The world record for a giant scoop was set in 1999 with strawberry ice cream weighing 7,800 pounds.

TIRAMISU

The largest tiramisu weighed 1,724 pounds and 14 ounces and was made by Colonia Italiana in Porrenturuy, Switzerland, on June 30, 2007.

TAMALE

In 2009 the record was set in Sacramento for the world's biggest tamale at 42 feet long and weighing 1,200 pounds.

TABBOULEH

The biggest tabbouleh, a typical Middle Eastern salad made of parsley, tomato, onion, and cracked wheat, was prepared in 2006 in the West Bank.

PAD THAI

Fifteen chefs cooked up the world's biggest dish of Pad Thai during the Thai Noodle Festival at a shopping center in Bangkok on June 3, 2004—it weighed 550 pounds and

was made with 330 pounds of noodles, 308 pounds of shrimp, and
840 eggs.

OLDEST SOUP

Chinese archaeologists unearthed a 2,400-year-old bowl of soup in Xi'an city.

OLDEST RESTAURANT

The world's oldest existing eatery opened in Kai-Feng, China, in 1153.

God's Gifts

8

Some things just can't be taught. Every so often, a person wins the genetic lottery and ends up with perfect pitch or the human body equivalent of a dolphin, making her literally a natural with music or Olympic swimming. Try as you might, you can either see letters and sounds as fireworks of color (despite its sinister name, synesthesia is not an infectious disease but actually pretty cool)—or you can't.

But not everything is perfect harmonizing and classical cheekbones—there are plenty of strange traits in the world. Consider the platypus. It may be ridiculous looking, but that duck-billed, flippered, egg-laying, poisonous marsupial is an amazing contrivance of the world. When things get weird they often get wonderful, too. Only a few people may be born with natural talents as numerous and diverse as a platypus's, but there are many people with wacky talents all around us. Remember that friend who never fails to show off her double-joints? Or that kid on the playground that would shake his pupils? Throw in a yoga mat, some milk, a stopwatch, and a yardstick and you could have had some natural-born record setters. With a little imagination (and if you've got the gift), it's that easy.

BIGGEST NOSE

At the past Long Nose World Championship in Langenbruck, Germany, Josef Dewold won the men's division with a nose measuring 4.8 inches, and Margot Sikora won the women's with a 4.1-inch nose.

MOST FINGERS AND TOES

An unidentified Chinese boy in Shenyang has fifteen fingers and sixteen toes, for a record total of thirty one.

SMALLEST GIRL IN THE WORLD

At 1 foot, 11 inches and fourteen years old, Jyoti Amge is the world's smallest girl.

HUMAN CALCULATOR

Alexis Lemaire, of London, took only 70.2 seconds to find the thirteenth root of a 200-digit randomly generated number.

YOUNGEST COMPUTER ENGINEER

M. Lavinashree of Tamilnadu, India, passed her Microsoft Certified Professional test at the age of eight.

OLDEST FATHER

With his fifty-four-year-old wife Shakuntala Devi, Ramajit Raghav sired his first child at the age of ninety-four, in India, in December 2010.

YOUNGEST YOGA INSTRUCTOR

Shruti Pandey became a yoga instructor at the age of five, having by that point learned all eighty-four positions and begun teaching classes.

YOUNGEST TATTOO ARTIST

Ruby Dickinson learned from her father how to safely ink tattoos at the age of three.

OLDEST FACEBOOK USER

Lillian Lowe, from Wales, United Kingdom, acquired a Facebook account at the age of 103.

MOST FERTILE MAN

Ziona Chana, the leader of a polygamous religious sect in India, has thirty-nine wives and ninety-four children, at a ratio of 2:41—along with thirty-three grandchildren, all living in one house.

YOUNGEST TO FLY A HOT AIR BALLOON SOLO

Bobby Bradley, at nine years old, launched his balloon on July 9, 2011.

FASTEST BABY

Nine-month-old Trent Miele crawled across a 10-foot mat in New York City in 18 seconds in August 2011.

LARGEST FAMILY

The Nigerian faith healer Bello Maasaba married 107 women and has fathered 185 children, though he has been divorced twenty-six times and fifty-two of his children have passed away.

YOUNGEST DRAG RACER

Belle Wheeler, at the age of twenty-three, passed her certifying test to drag race in September 2011, and shortly thereafter competed in a national race.

OLDEST ANGLER

Connie Laurie, an eighty-five-year-old from England, caught a marlin weighing more than 650 pounds in November 2011.

BIGGEST PENIS

Dr. Robert L. Dickenson measured the longest penis on reliable record, at 13.5 inches long and 6.25 inches in width—the man measured remains anonymous.

SMALLEST PENIS

Due to certain medical conditions, the smallest penis on record only measured 0.39 inches.

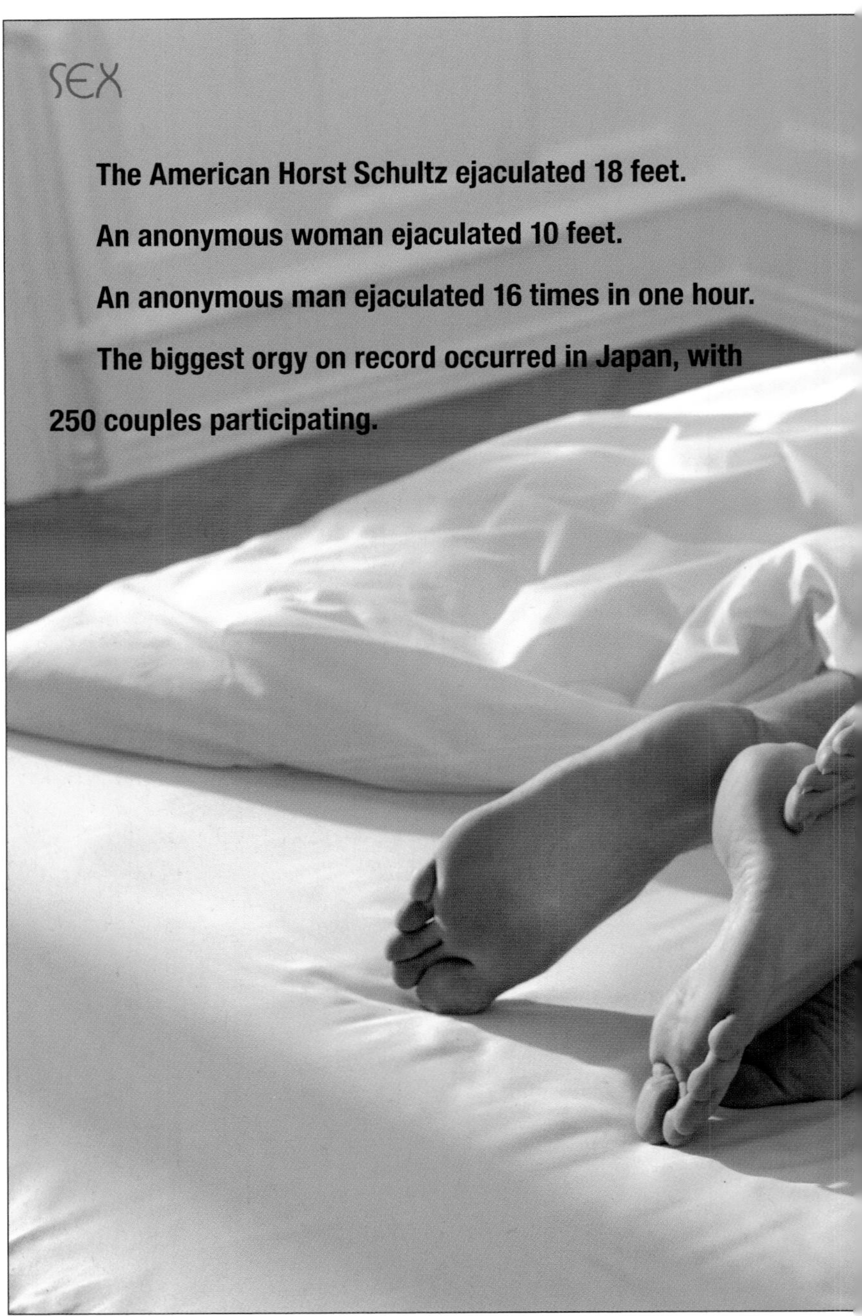

SEX

The American Horst Schultz ejaculated 18 feet.

An anonymous woman ejaculated 10 feet.

An anonymous man ejaculated 16 times in one hour.

The biggest orgy on record occurred in Japan, with 250 couples participating.

LARGEST VAGINA

A Scottish woman named Anna Swan was considered a giant, and gave birth to a baby whose head was 19 inches in circumference.

SMALLEST BABY

Olyviyanna Harbin-Page, born August 5, 2009, in Alabama, weighed only 9.1 ounces.

BLOWING BALLOONS WITH EARS

Wei Mingtang of Guilin, China, has blown out twenty candles in 20 seconds using air emitted through his ears; he can also blow balloons with them.

Miscellany

9

When searching the world for its most extreme and bizarre records, certain cases stand out as worthy of special notice. In other words, they defy categories even in a book on the weird and wacky—and so they're placed together as literally the odds and ends of this collection. These record-setters have made their marks in the most obscure niches and most unexpected corners, ranging from the Beta of video-game records to the Meta of record-holding records. These are the Great, Random Records of the "Weirdest and Wackiest"—enjoy!

LONGEST PALINDROME

Peter Norvig engineered a computer program to create the world's longest palindrome, with 17,259 words.

SHEEP SHEARING

Stacey Te Huia—on December 22, 2010, in Bennydale, New Zealand—sheared 603 strong-wooled sheep.

Cartwright Terry, on December 2, 2003, sheared 466 Merino Ewes in Western Australia.

DRESS OF YAK NIPPLES

Rachel Freire debuted a dress made of 3,000 yak nipples at London Fashion Week in September 2011.

MOST REPRODUCED WORK OF ART

The 1966 bust of Queen Elizabeth, sculpted by Arnold Machin, has been reproduced about 320 billion times.

BARREL ROLLING

A group of twenty-one people in Nuttlar, Germany, rolled a barrel 414 miles by hand, and in June 1981, they rolled a barrel of 50 liters of beer 5 miles.

Hartmut Vogel, Jurif Scneider, Udo Reinhold, Harry Fürch, Lothar Mätzhold, Detlef Bergmann, Torsten Kondziora, Lothar Baumann, and Dietmar Rudolf rolled a barrel of 100 liters 136 kilometers.

Jiří Plevka of the Czech Republic rolled a 50-liter barrel 50 meters in 12.9 seconds on April 25, 1988.

Marta Štěpánová of the Czech Republic rolled a 50-liter barrel 50 meters on April 25, 1988.

A team from Groningen, the Netherlands, rolled a 140-pound barrel 164 miles on November 29, 1998.

DRESS OF MOST HUMAN HAIR

Thelma Madine used 270 yards of hair extensions to create a dress that weighs 165 pounds in a size six.

FIRST TO BEAT *MARIO 64* WITH FEET

Wearing socks, "Vicas" beat *Super Mario 64* only using his feet, and acquiring every star, posting individual levels on his blog.

FERRET LEGGING

Frank Barlett of Staffordshire, England, kept a ferret in his pants for 5 hours and 30 minutes.

SPICIEST FLAG

The village of Daxinzhuang, China, created a massive flag entirely of hot peppers and corn cobs.

LONGEST NAME

Derek Parlane Stein Jackson Hunter McCloy Kennedy Scott Forsyth Henderson Boyd Robertson O'Hara Johnstone Miller Dawson Armour McDougall McLean McKean Fyfe McDonald Jardine Young Morris Denny Hamilton Watson Greig Wallace McQueen was given his 198-letter name by his father, after the Ranger's Football club's winning team of 1975.

COINS CAUGHT WITH ELBOW

"Pat," aka "Locococofreak," caught forty-seven pennies with his elbow in February 2009.

COFFEE AT THE HIGHEST ALTITUDE

Nidas Kiuberis, Grazvydas Vilcinskas, and Vytautas Samarinas, of Lithuania, jumped from an airplane and made coffee at a height of 20,000 feet, in August 2011.

FASTEST RUBIK'S CUBE ROBOT

A robot made by students at Swinburne University, can solve a Rubik's Cube in 10.18 seconds.

FASTEST DINING TABLE

Perry Watkins of Wingrave, England, has engineered a dining table averaging a speed of 99.06 mph.

June Gregg, of Ohio, has had the same bank account since 1913, and has recently turned 100 years old herself.

FASTEST COMPUTER

The "K Computer" in Japan can compute 8.162 quadrillion calculations per second.

SPACECRAFT

At a speed of 7,546 mph, an unmanned hypersonic Nasa X43 is the fastest aircraft ever.

LARGEST STICK BOMB REACTION

Tim Fort set off 6,767 stick-bombs on October 18, 2011

MOST MONKEY EMPLOYEES

The Kayabukiya Tavern, in Japan, employs a waitstaff of six monkeys.

FASTEST TRACTOR MOWER

Don Wales, of Wales, United Kingdom, built a lawn-mower that hit 86 mph.

FASTEST MOBILE HOME

The Goldschmitt Company custom-built a mobile home able to travel at 129 mph.

CAR SPEED

The world land speed record was set by Andy Green in 1992, driving the ThrustSSC up to a speed of 763 mph and becoming the first car to break the sound barrier.

FASTEST HANDICAP SCOOTER

A U.K. plumber Colin Furze broke the world record for fastest mobility scooter with a speed of 71.9 mph in 2010.

FASTEST SCHOOL BUS

Paul Stender, of Indianapolis, Indiana, built a bus capable of going up to 367 mph.

EMERGENCY EXIT

OLDEST CHEWING GUM

The world's oldest chewing gum was found by British archaeology students in Finland. The gum was discovered to be more than 5,000 years old.

LOUDEST BURP

Paula Hunn burped 104.9 decibels to set the world record for loudest burp.